THE WAR OF THE PACIFIC, 1879-1883

BY
GABRIELE ESPOSITO

ILLUSTRATED BY
ÁNGEL GARCÍA PINTO

Cover Art from Ángel García Pinto
The War of the Pacific, 1879-1883

This edition published in 2018

Published by Winged Hussar Publishing

1525 Hulse Road, Unit 1
Point Pleasant, NJ 08742

ISBN 978-1-945430-20-6

LCN 2018936805

Bibliographical References and Index
1. History. 2. South America. 3. Military

For more information on Winged Hussar Publishing, LLC, visit us at:
www.wingedhussarpublishing.com

TABLE OF CONTENTS

PREFACE

This book is dedicated to my parents, Maria Rosaria and Benedetto, for their immense love and great support during the creative process of the present work. Special thanks are due to Ángel García Pinto, for the eight magnificent uniform plates that illustrate this book. Another special mention is due to the editor of this volume, Vincent Rospond, for having enjoyed and sponsored this project since the early beginnings. Thanks to Winged Hussar Publishing the great public of military history fans is becoming always more interested and informed about South American wars and uniformology: I hope that this work will continue on the same line of my previous publications on Latina America, in order to stimulate the curiosity of even more international readers and attract them to the history of a tormented but magnificent continent.

The main aim of this book is to present a complete analysis of the organization, uniforms and weapons of the three South American armies involved in the War of the Pacific. For reasons of space, it has been impossible to include a complete narrative of the conflict: the main events of the war have been summarized in the chronology, in order to give the reader at least a general idea of the military operations. In any case, for more details about the War of the Pacific in general, see the detailed "Select bibliography" at the end of this work. Considering the enormous consequences that this war had on the history of South America, it is incredibly little-known outside the countries by which it was fought.

The War of the Pacific, fought during 1879-1883 between Chile and an alliance formed by Bolivia and Peru, was the largest military conflict ever fought in the Andean/Pacific region of South America. It was second only to the War of the Triple Alliance in terms of soldiers and casualties involved, being the most defining event in the history of the three nations that fought in it. The naval battles of the early phase of the conflict, as well as great field clashes like Tacna, Chorrillos and Miraflores, were among the greatest military events of their age. Their number of combatants was extremely large compared to usual South American standards. If the War of the Triple Alliance had been the "continental" war of that continent's eastern part, the War of the Pacific was its equivalent for the western part and for the Andean countries. The conflict studied in this book is also known as "Saltpetre War" or "Guano War", since it was mainly caused by the rivalry over possession of these two important natural resources [1]. Over centuries, the dry climate of the Peruvian and Bolivian Pacific coasts had permitted a vast accumulation of these two nitrates. Both were extremely important for the agriculture and industry of the time, since guano was used as a fertilizer and saltpetre had a fundamental role in the production of explosive. Possession of these two natural resources was the main cause of the war, but before giving more details regarding this question we should take into account some other political issues that were equally important in the process leading to the outbreak of hostilities. To do this we should go back to the early days of South American independence from Spain, when the three countries involved in the War of the Pacific were still young republics.

---

1 Sater, William F., *Andean Tragedy: Fighting the War of the Pacific 1879–1884*, University of Nebraska, 2007

During the Wars of Independence, Chile had been among the first South American countries to achieve autonomy from Spain; this objective was made possible thanks to the military help of Argentina (the leading independentist force in the southern half of the continent) and with the great military leadership of Chile's founding father Bernardo O'Higgins. Peru and Bolivia, instead, remained the strongest Spanish strongholds in Latin America until the end of the Liberation Wars. Bolivia in particular, at that time still known as "Upper Peru", was the starting point of all the repressive expeditions launched against Chile and Argentina by the Spanish Royal Army of Peru. Despite many difficulties and some significant internal divisions, the military forces of the two greatest South American liberators (Simón Bolivar and José de San Martín) were finally able to defeat the Spanish opposition and free Peru and Bolivia. Peru and its capital of Lima were liberated by an Argentine-Chilean Army led by San Martín and O'Higgins, while the last field battle for the independence of South America was won by Bolivar' forces in Bolivia (at Ayacucho, on 9 December 1824). The end of the Spanish Empire in the Americas, however, left many political questions unsettled between the new republics of the continent. The first and probably most significant of these regarded the status of the Upper Peru territory; on 6 August 1825 this proclaimed its independence as Bolivia under Bolivar's protection, but this political act was perceived in an extremely negative way by Peru. The Peruvians had always considered the Bolivian plateau as part of their national territory and thus could not accept its independence under military protection of a foreign country. In Bolivar's plans, the new country bearing his name was to act as centre of a new South American confederation, a sort of "United States of South America": for this reason, the "Liberator" could not renounce possession of Upper Peru and left part of his military forces to protect the territory. In 1828 the Peruvians launched a military campaign against the foreign garrison that occupied Bolivia, expelling it from the country: this action and a serious border dispute over the territory of Ecuador led to the outbreak of war between Gran Colombia and Peru. In 1829, after some months of land and naval conflict, the Confederation of Gran Colombia (Bolivar's political creature, formed by the union of Venezuela, Colombia and Ecuador) was finally able to defeat the Peruvians and secure possession of Ecuador's border territories. Bolivia, however, went definitively out from Bolivar's sphere of influence and no foreign garrison was to remain on its territory. By now a fully independent nation, it started its own history being autonomous from both Gran Colombia (which would break up in 1830) and Peru.

During the following decades both Peruvian and Bolivian elites continued to nurture political plans aiming at the unification of their two countries. These finally became reality with the creation of the Peru-Bolivian Confederation in 1836. This new union, however, generated resistance among several opposition groups in both countries and also among neighbouring states. Chile, in particular, opposed very strongly and since the beginning the new Confederation: the existence of such a powerful state on the Pacific coast of South America would have been a terrible menace for Chile's economy and independence. As a result of these conditions, the outbreak of war between Chile and the Confederation was just a question of time: the conflict started in 1836 and lasted until 1839, seeing an alliance formed by Chile, Argentina and Peruvian dissidents against the Confederation. The Argentine contribution to the alliance, however, was quite small and had very little consequences: Chile was practically left alone in its struggle against the larger northern enemy, but finally it was able to triumph on the field of battle and obtain the dissolution of the Peru-Bolivian Confederation. This "War of the Confederation" was nothing else than an anticipation of the future conflict fought exactly 40 years later. In 1841 the Peruvians tried to occupy Bolivia again but this time with a full-scale military invasion, which was repulsed by the recently reorganized Bolivian Army. A new and important phase had started in the policy of the Andean countries, which would lead to the escalation of 1879.

Admiral Juan Williams Rebolledo, commander of the Chilean Navy until August 1879.

INTRODUCTION

Since the early 1840's, guano and saltpetre started to be used on a massive scale and thus the demand for these two nitrates became increasingly larger[2]. During those same years Peru and Chile started to be opposed by a strong competition between their two most important ports: the Chilean one of Valparaiso and the Peruvian one of Callao. Being the largest ports and trading posts of the entire Pacific coast of South America, competition between them reflected the struggle between Chile and Peru over control of commerce in the western half of the continent. The greatest amounts of guano and saltpetre were located in the Desert of Atacama, a strategically important and large arid region mostly controlled by Bolivia. Possession of this border territory had been contested since the 1830's, because the Spanish colonial authorities had never defined a clear border between the territories that now formed Bolivia and Chile. Since the 1840's the Bolivian region of Antofagasta and the Peruvian one of Tarapacá (encompassing most of the Atacama Desert) had been populated and colonized by Chilean workers, who soon acquired a leading role in the new mining activities of the area. All the most important mines of the region soon fell in the hands of powerful Chilean companies, backed by their own government. The economic conquest of the Bolivian resources in the Atacama Desert was rapid and very profitable for the Chileans: the various Bolivian governments, in fact, did nothing to differentiate themselves from the foreigners who were taking away precious resources from their national territories. As we will see later, this situation changed only with the ascendancy of the Bolivian dictator Daza[3].

Another area of South America that was extremely rich of guano were the Chincha Islands, which belonged to Peru and produced almost 60% of the Peruvian government's annual revenue. In 1864 the Andean region was involved in a new war, fought for possession of these rich islands and of their strategic natural resources. The new Spanish Queen Isabella II wanted to reassert (albeit formally) her country's influence over the former South American colonies: for this reason, the Spaniards decided to launch a pre-emptive action and occupied the guano-rich Chincha Islands. The Spanish fleet easily blockaded all the principal Peruvian ports, disrupting commerce and fostering a high level of resentment throughout Latin America. Anti-Spanish sentiments increased in several South American countries, especially in Chile, Bolivia and Ecuador. It was clear to most observers that Spain had no intention of retaking the former colonies; however, Peru and the bordering countries still remained wary of any moves that might foreshadow an attempt to re-establish the Spanish Empire. Facing a formidable external threat, Chile decided to suspend its hostile behaviour towards Peru and sent ships with weapons and volunteers to aid the Peruvians.

As a consequence of these actions, what had started as a local conflict over possession of some islands transformed into a large war also known as "First War of the Pacific". After alliance with Peru, all the Chilean main ports were blockaded by the Spanish warships and the most important one of Valparaíso was

---

2 Lòpez-Urrutia, Carlos, *La Guerra del Pacifico 1879-1884*, Madrid, 2003
3 Sater, William F., *Andean Tragedy: Fighting the War of the Pacific 1879–1884*, University of Nebraska, 2007

bombarded. Chile's merchant fleet was destroyed in this action, with a total of 33 vessels being burned or sunk, and the port's facilities were heavily damaged. In 1866, the last year of the Chincha Islands War, Ecuador and Bolivia also declared war on Spain: this way all the ports on South America's Pacific coast became closed to the Spanish fleet. On 2 May of the same year the most important naval battle of the war took place, in front of the port of Callao. Both the Spaniards and the Peruvians who fought in it claimed victory, but it resulted in the withdrawal of the Spanish fleet from the Pacific. The conflict ended shortly afterwards, and the Chincha Islands were returned to Peru. The war had briefly united four South American countries against an ancient and common enemy, despite the political differences which traditionally divided them. The conflict had no important results from a political point of view but had significant military consequences especially for Chile. The war had been fought only at sea and the various naval operations showed how easily a relatively "small" Spanish fleet had been able to blockade the Chilean ports as well as how inadequate the Chilean Navy was. Many experts consider the defeats suffered during the Chincha Islands War (the bombardment of Valparaiso in particular) as the starting point for the ascendancy of the Chilean Navy as one of the best in the world.

In 1866, during the new political climate of mutual help, a treaty was ratified between Chile and Bolivia regarding the complex border issues of the Atacama Desert: according to it, the definitive border between Chile and Bolivia was to be the 24th parallel; the nitrates obtained by the mining of the area between parallels 23 and 25 would have been divided in equal parts between both countries. After all this treaty was quite positive for both nations, but it was not to last for long: in 1871 the Bolivian President Mariano Melgarejo, who had signed this agreement, lost power and was replaced by a new administration that was much more aggressive towards Chile. During the years that followed the Bolivians refused to pay the Chileans their fifty-percent of benefits derived from mining operations, thus leading to increasing tension between the two countries. As a result of this situation, in 1873 a Secret Treaty of Alliance was signed between Peru and Bolivia: this was mainly arranged to contrast the Chilean economic expansion, because many Peruvian and Bolivian politicians feared (correctly) that one day it would have transformed itself into a military one. This new military alliance would cause, six years later, the Peruvian involvement in the War of the Pacific. In 1874 a new agreement was signed between Chile and Bolivia in order to avoid a direct military confrontation, according to which the Chileans relinquished all the economic benefits already matured but never obtained in exchange for the Bolivian promise of not raising taxes for 25 years on the Chilean mining companies already installed on Bolivian territory[4]. In 1876 all the three Andean countries changed leadership. The new President of Chile was Pinto, an intelligent man who was strongly influenced in his foreign policy by the powerful mining companies. In Peru the new president was Prado, elected as usual in Peru after a long series of internal struggles and political assassinations. During the previous years the country had been divided into two main political factions: the traditional military one and the new one of the "civilistas". The first wanted to maintain its control over the state, which had been strong and unopposed since independence of Peru; the emerging faction of the reformist "civilistas", instead, wanted a civil government for Peru. Prado was himself a general, a popular hero of the Chincha Islands War against Spain, but his election was the result of a compromise between the two factions: in fact, his political line was not as rigid as that of previous military rulers.

The situation in Bolivia was similar to that of Peru, albeit with some important differences regarding the leadership. Daza, the new military dictator, was the typical South American "caudillo" of those times: he came from a poor family and had enlisted in the Bolivian Army when very young. He had gradually increased his personal power in the ranks of the armed forces to the point of becoming commander of the

---

4 Lòpez-Urrutia, Carlos, *La Guerra del Pacifico 1879-1884*, Madrid, 2003

The monitor Huáscar as it is today, after complete restoration.

"Colorados" Battalion (the most important unit of the Bolivian Army). In 1876 he was promoted General and subsequently revolted against the legitimate president. Thanks to the help of the "Colorados" he was able to seize absolute power with a military coup and started to rule as a ferocious military ruler: the first action of his presidency was that of using the remnants of the national treasure to pay the "Colorados". Every kind of opposition to his decisions was considered illegal and many political opponents were simply killed without process. With Daza's rise to power there was also an increase of Bolivian nationalism, especially against the Chileans who were "robbing" natural resources belonging to the Bolivian people. On 10 February 1879 a new tax on the nitrates, known as the "Ten Cents Tax", was approved by the National Congress of Bolivia (as ordered by Daza). This new tax was a clear violation of the 1874 treaty between Chile and Bolivia, because with it the Bolivian government had accepted to not raise taxes on the nitrates for 25 years. Daza did know this very well and thus ordered the creation of this new tax as a clear provocation to Chile. The Chilean companies refused to pay and appealed to their country for protection of their rights: Daza responded with an order to auction all the Bolivian nitrate mines that were in Chilean hands, well knowing the consequences of this act of open hostility. The Bolivian dictator was sure that he could count on the support of Peru thanks to the Secret Treaty of 1873 and was also sure that Argentina would have joined the alliance. This prevision was not so unrealistic: in those years serious border tensions were taking place between Argentina and Chile over control of Patagonia (both countries wanted to expand in that region and their interests were contrasting). Argentina, however, remained neutral and resolved the border issue with Chile using diplomacy. On 12 February 1879, two days before the fixed date for auction of the nitrate mines, Chile broke off diplomatic relations with Bolivia.

CHRONOLOGY OF THE WAR OF THE PACIFIC

• May 4, 1876: Hilarión Daza seizes power as dictator of Bolivia after a military coup.

• August 2, 1876: Mariano Prado becomes new President of Peru.

• September 18, 1876: Anibal Pinto is elected new President of Chile.

• February 10, 1879: The National Congress of Bolivia approves the new "Ten Cents Tax" on nitrate extraction, as ordered by Daza.

• February 12, 1879: Chile breaks diplomatic relations with Bolivia and starts preparations for war.

• February 14, 1879: A Chilean military expedition under command of Colonel Sotomayor lands at Antofagasta with the main task of seizing control of the strategic port and of preventing Bolivian actions against Chilean goods (on that day Chilean mines were to be auctioned).

• March 1, 1879: Bolivia declares war on Chile. All the Chileans living on Bolivian territory are expulsed from the country and their goods are confiscated.

• March 1879: Peru attempts a diplomatic mediation between Bolivia and Chile in order to avoid a direct military confrontation. Meanwhile the existence of the Secret Treaty of Mutual Defence between Peru and Bolivia is discovered by the Chileans, leading to failure of the Peruvian diplomatic efforts. Chilean soldiers advance from Antofagasta without meeting any kind of Bolivian opposition: by the end of the month all the contested area between parallels 23 and 24 is occupied. The Chilean advance stops at the southern border of Peru: Bolivia has no more access to the Pacific Ocean.

• April 1, 1879: Chile declares war on Bolivia and Peru. Beginning of the War of the Pacific.

• April 5, 1879: The Chilean Navy starts the blockading of the important southern Peruvian port of Iquique. Given the few usable roads and railroad lines, Chile had no possibility to move a large army against Peru across the arid regions of the Atacama Desert. The only way to attack southern Peru was that of disembarking troops on the enemy coast which was located north of the arid regions. Before doing this, however, the Chileans had to achieve total naval superiority by destroying the Peruvian Navy. As a result of this situation the first months of the conflict were fought only at sea. In theory, there was no great difference in the quality and number of warships between the two enemy navies (Bolivia had no fleet). The Chilean naval power, built up after the disasters of the Chincha Islands War, was based on the two twin warships "Cochrane" and "Blanco Encalada", excellent central-battery ironclads that had been commissioned in England during 1874 and 1875. In addition to these there were the modern corvettes "Chacabuco" and "O'Higgins", the older corvettes "Esmeralda" and "Abtao", the gunboat "Magallanes" (built in England in 1874) and the schooner "Covadonga" (captured from the Spaniards during the Chincha Islands War). The Peruvian Navy relied mainly on the broadside ironclad "Independencia" (commissioned in 1860) and on the monitor "Huáscar", the only real modern warship of the fleet. It had been commissioned in England in 1866, for use in the war against Spain. The Peruvian Navy comprised also the corvette "Unión" (the fastest military ship then in the Pacific), the gunboat "Pilcomayo" and the coastal monitors "Atahualpa" and "Manco Cápac" (bought from the USA as surplus of the Civil War, being originally named "Catawba" and "Oneota"). What made the Chilean Navy far superior than the Peruvian one was the quality of its officers and seamen, who were better trained and disciplined than their Peruvian equivalents. From a technical point of view, the Chileans had many advantages over the Peruvians: their ironclads had twice the armour of the Peruvian ships and a greater range and hitting power. In addition to this, Chilean warships used the excellent armour-piercing Palliser shots, which proved to be decisive in the following naval battles. Chile could also count on better facilities, since Peru had no naval arsenals where to repair the damaged ships.

Contemporary photo of the Chilean fleet at the beginning of the war.

• April 12, 1879: Indecisive naval engagement of Chipana, the first real military action of the war.

• May 21, 1879: Naval Battle of Iquique; the Peruvians remove the Chilean blockade of the port, but loose their biggest warship (the ironclad "Independencia"). The Peruvian "Huáscar" sinks the Chilean "Esmeralda".

• June-October 1879: The Peruvian monitor "Huáscar", under command of Admiral Miguel Grau, makes several incursions into Chilean waters, challenging the enemy navy's domination along the entire Chilean coast. The warship attacked many ports, captured transports and, despite being always outnumbered, held off the Chilean Navy for four consecutive months. Miguel Grau's brilliant victories with the "Huáscar" upheld the Peruvian morale and terrorized the Chilean public opinion, preventing the entire Chilean Navy from taking control of the sea and any attempt to disembark troops on the Peruvian territory. One of Grau's most important achievements was the capture of the transport ship "Rímac", having a squadron of the "Carabineros de Yungay" on board.

Painting showing the sinking of the Chilean "Esmeralda" during the battle of Iquique.

• October 8, 1879: After four months of chase, the Chilean fleet finally catches up with the "Huáscar" at the Battle of Angamos. During this action the Chilean warships "Cochrane", "Blanco Encalada", "O'Higgins" and "Covadonga" engaged battle with the Peruvian "Huáscar" and "Unión". The shots of the "Huáscar" had no effects on the armour of the enemy ships, while the Chilean grenades nearly destroyed Grau's warship. After several hours of bitter fighting, the Chileans managed to capture the "Huáscar" despite a final attempt by the remaining Peruvian crew to scuttle the ship. Grau died during the fighting, with 35 of his men. The heroic Admiral, who forced Chile to shift its fleet from the blockading of ports to the hunting of his warship, is still celebrated today as the most important personality in the history of the Peruvian Navy (one of the latter's most prestigious decorations being the "Order of Great Admiral Grau"). The victory of Angamos gave the Chileans complete control of the sea, since the remaining Peruvian warships avoided confrontation with the Chilean ships for the rest of the conflict. This way the Chilean Navy would later start its blockade of Callao and support with no difficulties the various landings of land forces.

• November 2, 1879: A Chilean invading force of 10,000 soldiers disembarks on the southern Peruvian coast at Pisagua. After a few hours of battle the important Peruvian port/city is conquered by the Chileans and the Allied defenders are defeated.

• November 6, 1879: Cavalry skirmish of Pampa Germania; the Peruvian and Bolivian cavalrymen are defeated.

Painting showing the crucial moments of the decisive naval clash at Angamos.

• November 19, 1879: Battle of Dolores/San Francisco. Some days after the landings, a column of about 6,000 Chilean soldiers left the city of Pisagua under command of Colonel Sotomayor to continue the offensive. To stop the Chileans, the Allies grouped a total of 11,000 soldiers under command of General Buendía. Sotomayor occupied a near prominence known as "Hill of San Francisco", with the idea of fighting a defensive battle against the numerically superior enemy force. The Allies attacked the Chilean positions, but after some hours of bitter fighting the Chileans launched a decisive counterattack. The Allied cavalry fled from the battlefield without covering the general retreat, which soon became a rout. The outcome of the battle was a great Chilean victory: the Allies lost a huge amount of war materials such as cannons, ammunition and weapons. The Chileans lost only 200 men, while the Allies had a total of 3.300 casualties.

• November 27, 1879: Battle of Tarapacá. After the severe defeat of Dolores/San Francisco, Buendía managed to regroup only a part of his soldiers and then decided to join the other Peruvian forces located in the city of Tarapacá. While in the important city, the Allies received some reinforcements that increased their total number to 4,500 men. The Chileans, who did not know of these reinforcements, had sent only a small force of 2,000 soldiers to pursue the defeated enemy. The battle between the two opposing forces was fought in the ravine of San Lorenzo de Tarapacá. The ensuing fight was absolutely cruel, without either side asking for or giving quarter. Control of the ravine continuously changed hands during the battle. At the end of the day the Chileans abandoned their positions and their fragmented forces were forced to retire, leaving the field in Peruvian hands. The Peruvians had achieved their first victory of the war, with 500 casualties; the Chileans had lost 700 soldiers and 10 field guns. During the following night the Peruvian Army marched to Arica and abandoned its positions at Tarapacá: with this strategic mistake it lost all the advantages gained during the previous day.

• December 23, 1879: The Peruvian President Prado is deposed by an internal revolution led by Nicolás de Piérola, who becomes dictator of Peru thanks to great popular support. Piérola had already attempted a coup against Prado in 1877 but had been defeated by the legitimate government thanks to the support of the Royal Navy. After being exiled, he returned to Peru in 1879 to launch a new revolution (this time more successful).

• December 28, 1879: Daza is deposed as dictator of Bolivia after a military coup supported by the public opinion and led by Colonel Camacho (who took the leadership away from Daza).

• January-February 1880: Preparations for the second war campaign. The Chileans are ready to attack the Peruvian provinces of Arica and Tacna.

• February 26, 1880: An army of 13,000 Chileans disembarks on the Peruvian coast at Ilo, north of the Tacna and Arica provinces. The Chilean high command has avoided a difficult march across the Atacama Desert, landing its forces north of the enemy thanks to a decisive naval superiority. The Allied forces made no attempts to resist.

• March 22, 1880: During the march towards the city of Tacna, the Chilean Army attacks the Peruvian stronghold located on Los Ángeles hill. This position, defended by 1,400 men and placed on the left flank of the advancing Chileans, was considered to be impregnable. After some hours of bitter fighting the Chilean flag is placed on top of the hill.

• May 26, 1880: Battle of Alto de la Alianza/Tacna. A total of 14,000 Allied soldiers, commanded by the Bolivian Narciso Campero, faced a Chilean force of 10,000 men led by Manuel Baquedano. The Allies, entrenched in strong defensive positions located east of Tacna, are finally defeated after several hours of bloody fighting and terrible Chilean attacks. Casualties are very heavy on both sides (5,500

Clash between Chilean and Peruvian soldiers at the battle of Arica (7 June 1880).

for the Allies and 2,000 for the Chileans), but Baquedano achieves complete victory in the second war campaign. The province of Tacna is in Chilean hands. After this terrible defeat the remnants of the Bolivian Army decided to retreat back to their country: Bolivia will remain at war with Chile until the final defeat of the Peruvians in 1884, but from this moment on the Bolivian military forces will remain in their country (thus playing no further role in any kind of military operation).

• June 7, 1880: The city of Arica, the last Peruvian bastion in the south, is conquered by a force of 4,000 Chilean soldiers. The second war campaign is over.

• June-November 1880: At this point of the war the military operations had a long stop, because the Chileans had occupied all the territories that were rich of nitrates (the Bolivian province of Antofagasta and the Peruvian ones of Tarapacá, Tacna and Arica). The Allies, in complete disarray and with no military forces available, had no options but to wait for the moves of their enemy. A series of peace talks, inspired by the USA, took place during October 1880: these, known as the "Lackawanna Conference" from the name of the US warship on which they took place, lasted five days but came to nothing. The Allies did not accept relinquishing control of the Antofagasta and Tarapacá provinces, demanded by Chile as indemnification for the war expenses. Their refusal put an end to the peace conference and the conflict continued. The Chileans could have been satisfied with their territorial conquests, but the strong pressure of the public opinion and the expansionist ambitions of the National Congress obliged President Pinto to continue the war until the "complete extermination of the enemy". As a result, the Chilean high command soon planned a new campaign with the objective of obtaining an unconditioned surrender of Peru. The target of the new offensive, which had to be decisive for the sorts of the war, was the same Peruvian capital of Lima.

• November-December 1880: The shortage of shipping precluded an immediate landing at Lima and thus the Chileans decided to disembark at Pisco (200 miles south of the Peruvian capital). On 20 November, 8,800 men landed at Pisco and captured the city from its 3,000 defenders. After securing control of the Ica province (surrounding Pisco), the Chileans disembarked the rest of their forces during the following weeks (3,500 men on 2 December and 14,000 men on 15 December). At this point, before advancing on Lima, Baquedano decided that only one brigade of the army would have marched north:

The USS warship "Lackawanna", on which indecisive peace talks took place in 1880.

this elite force, commanded by Patricio Lynch, had the order to occupy the coastal town of Chilca (located just 28 miles south of Lima). The rest of the Chilean Army would have been embarked again, landing at Chilca only after its occupation by Lynch. Everything went as planned by Baquedano and by 22 December the entire Chilean Army was already in the valley of Lurín, on the southern outskirts of Lima. Meanwhile Piérola had completely reorganized the Peruvian military forces, which were now structured into the "Army of the Line" and "Army of the Reserve". The Peruvian dictator also ordered the construction of two parallel defensive lines south of Lima, one at Chorrillos and one at Miraflores. The "Army of the Line" was deployed on the line of Chorrillos, while the "Army of the Reserve" had to defend the line of Miraflores. The first line of defence was extremely strong: it ran from the seaside of Chorrillos through four hills (Morro Solar, Santa Teresa, San Juan and Pamplona) until Monterrico Chico. This line was approximately 15 km long and was defended by guns, covering forts, landmines and trenches located along the top of the steeply natural hills. The second line of Miraflores was less strong than that of Chorrillos, consisting of 7 redoubts distributed on 12 km. It extended from the beach of Miraflores until the Surco River, being divided in three main sectors.

• January 13, 1881: Battle of Chorrillos. The positions of the Peruvian "Army of the Line", defended by 22,000 men, are attacked by the Chilean Army with 23,000 soldiers. After a day of harsh fighting, during which both sides showed great valour, the Chileans were finally able to break the Peruvian line of defence and defeat the enemy in a decisive way. The Peruvians lost more or less 8,000 of their best soldiers, while Baquedano's losses amounted to 3,300 men. After the battle a truce was declared while negotiations took place; the Chileans wished to avoid another battle before entering Lima, but the talks quickly broke down.

• January 15, 1881: Battle of Miraflores. The second Peruvian defensive line, protected by 14,000 men (reservists or survivors from the previous battle), was invested by a total of 12,000 Chileans. In the initial phase of the clash the defenders were very near to victory, but in the end Baquedano's men were able to break the enemy defences and caused a complete rout of the Peruvians. Chilean losses amounted to 2,000 men, while Peruvian casualties numbered 5,000. The two great battles for Lima were over and the third was campaign had ended. During the night of the following day (16 January) Lima became victim of civil unrest and rioting, caused by the constant flow of disbanded soldiers and deserters coming from the southern defensive lines; as a result, Baquedano received a formal request from Lima's mayor to occupy the city with his troops as soon as possible and restore order.

• January 17, 1881: Lima opens its gates to the Chileans, who took complete possession of the city. Piérola had already abandoned his capital, with the intention of continuing resistance in the other provinces of Peru.

Admiral Patricio Lynch, commander of the Chilean occupation forces in Peru.

• February-July 1881: Soon after the Chilean occupation of Lima, resistance forces had started to be active in the Andes of central Peru (from February 1881). In April the supreme commander of the Chilean occupation forces, Admiral Lynch, decided to launch a first punitive expedition against the "guerrillas" in the Andes. The Chileans had to defeat any last attempt of resistance in order to conclude the war, since the Peruvians had not surrendered after the crushing defeats of January. The fourth war campaign, starting from April 1881, is known as "La Breña" or "Sierra" Campaign: its name derives from the great Peruvian mountain range, the central Andes, where most of the fighting took place. It was a harsh and cruel fight, during which both sides committed several atrocities. Meanwhile the political situation in Peru was extremely confused: after Piérola's escape from Lima, the Chileans had formed a new government led by Francisco García-Calderón, which

General Baquedano, commander of the Chilean Army from April 1880 to May 1881.

Contemporary photo showing the entrance of the Chilean infantry in Lima.

was supposed to be a collaborationist one having the task of administrating the Peruvian territories under Chilean occupation. Piérola and his officers, including the new leader of the resistance forces General Cáceres, did not recognize the authority of the new collaborationist president. As a result of all the above, a first Chilean expedition with 700 men was sent to the central Andes on 15 April 1881: this was commanded by Colonel Letelier, who had orders to conduct a severe counter-insurgency campaign. Very soon the expedition transformed into a savage looting of the local villages, with many abuses being committed over the civilian population. At the same time Letelier's soldiers achieved very little results in their chase of the Peruvian resistance forces. The harsh repression augmented the hostile feelings of the Peruvian mountaineers towards the Chileans and resulted in heavy attacks during their retreat to Lima. The expedition had been a total failure: Letelier and his officers were court-martialled for embezzlement, while Cáceres gained more time to gather and organize new resistance forces. The Chileans were now condemned to face a long guerrilla war.

• September 28, 1881: After months of indecisive negotiations, the Chileans decided to remove Calderón as chief of the Peruvian government: instead of being leader of the collaborationists, he had showed a great patriotic spirit (unexpected by the Chileans) by opposing the territorial claims advanced by the invaders. Calderón, before being sent in exile to Chile, named Admiral Lizardo Montero as his successor. Montero had a strong will to continue the fight and thus was soon recognized as legitimate president by Cáceres. Piérola, having gradually lost support of the population after the fall of Lima, abandoned Peru. Montero, now having undisputed leadership, later moved to the southern city of Arequipa and took command of the local garrison. Arequipa, the most important city of the south, was still in Peruvian hands: after the Battle of Tacna, the remnants of the Peruvian forces moved to the city and were now entrenched in it. They had remained inactive during the third campaign of the war, simply acting as normal military garrison of the city. The Chileans, employing all their forces against Lima, did not plan any operation against Arequipa since its garrison (albeit large) was not considered to be a menace. This situation remained the same also after Montero's arrival, because the "Army of Arequipa" took no military initiatives.

Colonel Estanislao del Canto, commander of the first Chilean expedition in the "Sierra".

• January-July 1882: Pressed by the Chilean National Congress and public opinion, Lynch absolutely needed to achieve a definitive victory over the resistance forces of Cáceres. The Peruvian "guerrillas" were by now more aggressive and organized, mainly thanks to the general support received by the population and local Church. Cáceres had his headquarters at Chosica, not far from Lima, and was a constant menace for the Chileans. At the beginning of January two Chilean divisions marched from

Lima with the objective of attacking Cáceres at Chosica, but by the time the Chileans arrived the Peruvians had already abandoned the position. During January and February, the Chileans pursued Cáceres in his retreat across the Andes, but the outcome of these operations was not decisive. The Chileans achieved some minor victories, but the Peruvians organized several effective ambushes against them. The Chilean forces, under command of Colonel Estanislao del Canto, were by now scattered through the Peruvian Andes and divided into small garrisons that were stationed in several villages. The Chilean soldiers endured a severe lack of supplies including food, clothes, shoes and ammunitions; in addition, they suffered heavy casualties from mountain sickness, typhus and frostbite. When the situation turned desperate, Colonel del Canto went to Lima in order to request authorization to retreat: after receiving it, the difficult operation started. This new expedition to the Andes was soon a failure: the plan was now to evacuate the Chilean forces by gathering up the scattered garrisons successively as the main column left the mountains. One of these, numbering just seventy-seven men who were garrisoning the village of Concepción, was completely wiped out on 9 July. After 27 hours of bitter fighting against 1,300 Peruvian irregulars, all the Chilean defenders were killed. The defeat suffered at Concepción, plus two other ones at Marcavalle and Pucará, convinced the Chilean high command that the central Andes had to be completely abandoned. After victory at the clash of Tarmatambo (15 July 1882), the remnants of the Chilean forces were finally able to retreat back to Lima (entering the city at the beginning of August). While all these events took place in the central Andes, in the north another nucleus of resistance was active since some months. Miguel Iglesias, one of Piérola's most important supporters and an important Peruvian military commander, had left Lima after its capture from the Chileans and had taken refuge in his large estates that were located in the northern province of Cajamarca. There he started to organize some resistance forces recruited from the inhabitants of his land properties. In February 1882 Lizardo Montero, as President of Peru, nominated Iglesias supreme commander of the northern provinces: having this new political role, Iglesias led his small force of 600 men against the Chileans at San Pablo (13 July 1882), obtaining a minor victory. Shortly after this success, however, Iglesias' small army was defeated by the Chileans and the province of Cajamarca was occupied and sacked by the foreign invaders. After this defeat Iglesias became strongly convinced that peace with Chile was the only realistic way to save Peru from total destruction and completely changed his political attitude.

• August 1882-February 1883: Convinced that any further resistance against the Chileans had no hope of success, Iglesias issued a manifesto calling for peace, known as "Grito de Montán" (31 August 1882); this, however, was rejected by Cáceres and Montero who continued to fight against the Chileans. At this point Iglesias decided to continue on his way and started official peace talks with the Chileans, after proclaiming himself Supreme Commander of Peru. To have some legitimacy at the eyes of the Peruvian people, in December 1882 he called a convention of political representatives from the seven departments of northern Peru; on 1st January 1883 the northern representatives proclaimed Iglesias "Regenerating President of Peru" and gave him the charge of concluding a definitive peace treaty with the Chileans. The latter soon understood that Iglesias was the only possible interlocutor who could help them to achieve a positive end of the conflict: for this reason, they started to officially support him since February 1883. Iglesias was considered as a traitor by the majority of the Peruvians, while Cáceres' popularity as national hero was at its peak.

• March-June 1883: The only way that the Chileans had to legitimate the collaborationist government of Iglesias was that of defeating once and for all the resistance forces of Cáceres; this way, after years of war far from home, they would have been able to conclude a very favourable peace treaty with a puppet Peruvian government. As a consequence of the above, Lynch decided to send a new expedition against Cáceres: this new force, comprising three divisions, was very well armed and equipped. The Chileans had learned a lot from their previous failures in the Andes and now the expedition was prepared with extreme accuracy. The basic plan of the Chilean high command was that of surrounding the Peruvian resistance forces and obliging them to fight in a conventional field battle. By the third week of June the Peruvians were in a critical position: Cáceres had two Chilean divisions in close pursuit on the back and another one attempting to block him from the opposite direction. He ordered a desperate retreat of his forces via the Llankanuku pass, located at an altitude of over 6,000 meters: thanks to this risky manoeuvre, however, Cáceres managed to evade the main Chilean force.

• July 10, 1883: Battle of Huamachuco. On 5 July the Peruvian forces had arrived near Huamachuco, where they learned that the third Chilean division of Colonel Gorostiaga was in the town. Seeing an opportunity to destroy one of the Chilean divisions that were pursuing him, Cáceres called a war council and the decision was taken to stop retreating and try to destroy the Chilean forces occupying Huamachuco. As soon as he saw the Peruvians on the top of the surrounding hills, Colonel Gorostiaga immediately gathered all his troops and evacuated the city, taking position on the nearby Sazón hill (a perfect defensive position with some Inca ruins on the top). On the early hours of 10 July, the 2,000 men of Cáceres attacked the 1,700 Chileans of Gorostiaga. After some bitter fighting, Gorostiaga's forces were reduced to defending themselves on the top of the Sazón hill and Peruvian victory seemed imminent. At this point Cáceres made a fatal mistake: he ordered to his small artillery to relocate into the valley facing the hill, in order to provide the final coup to the Chilean positions. Gorostiaga saw this tactical error and ordered a cavalry charge: the defenceless Peruvian artillery was completely annihilated; seven guns were lost, while the artillerymen were all dispersed or killed. Meanwhile, the Chileans quickly reorganized themselves and launched a massive bayonet counter-attack against the Peruvians. The Chilean downhill counter-attack broke the enemy lines and Cáceres' men started to flee from the battlefield. With this decisive victory the Chileans had practically won the War of the Pacific: the resistance forces of Cáceres had lost 800 men (many of them officers) and thus were in no conditions to continue any effective resistance.

• October 20, 1883: Signing of the Peace Treaty of Ancón between the Chileans and Iglesias' government, end of the hostilities between Chile and Peru. According to the treaty, Peru ceded forever the province of Tarapacá to Chile and the Chileans were also to occupy the provinces of Tacna and Arica for the following 10 years; after this period of time a plebiscite was to be held to determine the nationality of the two provinces. During the following decades the two countries failed to agree on the terms of this plebiscite; in 1929, through US mediation, the definitive Treaty of Lima was signed between the two parts to resolve this political issue. According to the new treaty Chile kept Arica and Peru re-acquired Tacna.

• October 29, 1883: The garrison of Arequipa, commanded by Lizardo Montero, surrenders to the Chileans without fighting after a revolt of the population. The legitimate Peruvian President is obliged to abandon the city and flees to Bolivia.

• April 4, 1884: Signing of a definitive truce between Chile and Bolivia. According to it the entire province of Antofagasta was given to Chile and Bolivia lost its access to the Pacific. A real peace treaty between the two countries was signed only in 1904: this new "Treaty of Peace and Friendship" confirmed Chilean possession of Antofagasta, but in return Chile agreed to build the Arica–La Paz railway (a strategic railroad connecting the Bolivian capital with the port of Arica) and guaranteed freedom of transit for Bolivian commerce through Chilean territory and ports.

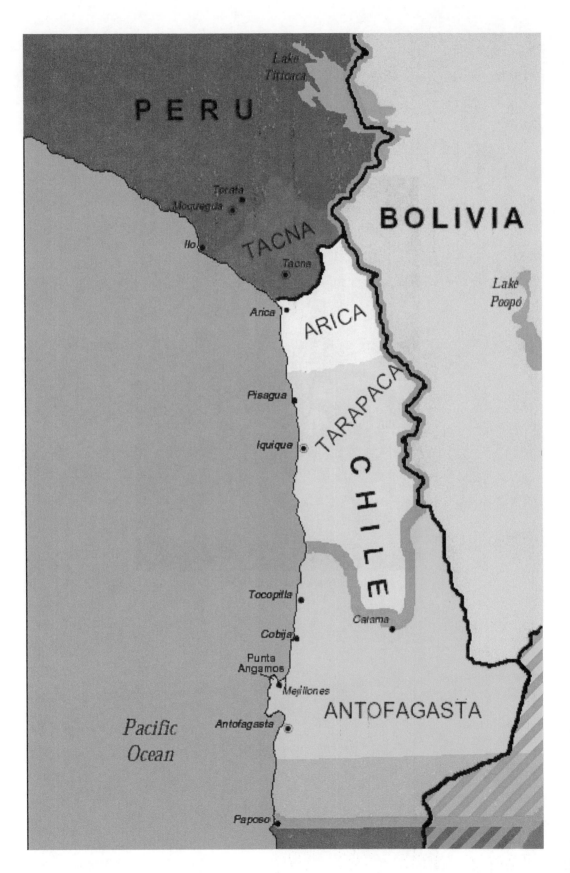

Hilarion Daza Groselle

THE BOLIVIAN ARMY

ORGANIZATION

Similarly, to the Peruvian one, the pre-war Bolivian Army had too many officers who commanded too few men: in fact, at the beginning of the hostilities, the Bolivian armed forces consisted of just 1,700 men, of whom 810 were officers or NCOs . Approximately there was an officer for each three rankers or NCOs[5]. The structure of the land forces comprised three infantry battalions, two cavalry squadrons and one regiment of artillery:

- 1st Line Infantry Battalion "Daza", also known as "1st Grenadiers of the Guard"

- 2nd Line Infantry Battalion "Sucre", also known as "2nd Grenadiers of the Guard"

- 3rd Line Infantry Battalion "Illimani", also known as "1st Cazadores of the Guard"

- Line Cavalry Squadron "Bolívar", also known as "1st of Hussars"

- Line Cavalry Squadron "Escolta", also known as "1st of Cuirassiers"

- Artillery Regiment "Santa Cruz"

Each of the three infantry battalions was dressed in one of the colours from Bolivia's national flag: the 1st in red, the 2nd in yellow and the 3rd in green. For this reason, the three units were commonly known by their popular nicknames, which were respectively "Colorados", "Amarillos" and "Verdes" ("Reds", "Yellows" and "Greens"). The organization reported above had changed quite little since 1860, when Colonel Placido Yañez had reorganized the Bolivian forces after the cruel civil war of 1857. It was in 1860 that the 1st Infantry Battalion received for the first time its red uniform, despite the fact that Bolivian military units were generally dressed in national colours since the presidency of José Ballivián (1841–47), who had secured Bolivia's autonomy from Peru by defeating the Peruvian Army at the Battle of Ingavi in 1841 and who had completely re-founded the Bolivian armed forces after the dissolution of the Peru-Bolivian Confederation (in existence during 1836-1839). After the installation of General Mariano Melgarejo as dictator of Bolivia in 1864, the Bolivian Army had gradually transformed into a small "private" force that acted as personal police of the dictator. It was Melgarejo, for example, who formed the "Cuirassiers" Cavalry Regiment as his personal mounted escort; the men from this unit were all fanatic supporters of his cause and their officers were extremely loyal to the dictator (having helped him in his violent ascendancy to power). After the fall of Melgarejo a new unit did take the responsibility to perform escort duties for the Bolivian Presidents, but the "Cuirassiers" survived and later transformed into Daza's "Escolta" Squadron.

---

5 Sater, William F., *Andean Tragedy: Fighting the War of the Pacific 1879–1884*, University of Nebraska, 2007

The 1st Infantry Battalion "Colorados" was with no doubts the most important unit of the pre-war Bolivian Army: it had initially been formed during the civil war of 1857, being later transformed by Colonel Placido Yañez into an elite unit. The latter imposed a strict discipline over the battalion, which received better training and equipment than any other Bolivian military unit. It soon became a sort of "praetorian guard", which loyalty was fundamental for each Bolivian president or dictator who held power during those years. The "Colorados", thanks to the preferential treatment received, usually enlisted taller and stronger men than the other infantry units; in addition, at the outbreak of the war in 1879, all the soldiers of the unit were armed with the excellent M1871 Remington rolling-block rifle. It was thanks to the decisive support of the "Colorados" that Daza became dictator of Bolivia in 1876, by defeating the military forces loyal to President Morales, and installed himself as absolute ruler of the country. After Daza's ascendancy, the privileges of the "Colorados" became even more apparent: of the 593 men forming the unit, 370 had ranks above that of common soldier and thus received higher pay. Knowing this, it is easy to understand why the Bolivian Army had such an excessive number of officers and NCOs. The dictator was able to rule the country only thanks to the help of his elite battalion, which gradually became a sort of "familiar" unit: in fact, by 1879, most of the soldiers from the "Colorados" were relatives or personal friends of Daza.

The "Sucre" Battalion had been formed in 1876, after Daza came to power, with policemen coming from Sucre and Potosí; it was considered the best unit of the army after the "Colorados de Daza". The "Illimani" Battalion, also formed in 1876, despite having the denomination of "Cazadores" (light infantry) was equipped, armed and trained exactly like the other two line infantry units. Both the 2nd and 3rd Battalion of infantry numbered around 300 men each, so they had a lower establishment than the "Colorados". The 1st Cuirassiers, also known as "Escolta" Squadron, was the mounted equivalent of the "Colorados": it provided Daza's personal mounted escort and bore several vainglorious nicknames, like "The Tigers of Bengal", "The Immortals" or "The Tenth Legion of Caesar" [6]. In many respects it was nothing more than a local version of Napoleon III's elite "Cent-Gardes". At the beginning of the war this unit numbered more or less 130 men. The 1st Hussars, the other Bolivian cavalry unit existing before the war, was not a merely ceremonial corps like the "Cuirassiers": in fact, it was the only real cavalry force of the Bolivian Army. It numbered 30 officers and 251 men who, differently from the Cuirassiers, were heavily involved into the military operations of the first war campaign. As is clear from the denominations of the units that made up the pre-war Bolivian Army, of which four out of six were known as "of the Guard" or "Escort", the Bolivian armed forces were a small and very personal army, strongly linked to Daza: but they were not a professional and modern force that could fight with success in a large-scale war.

On 20 February 1879, Daza was informed of the Chilean occupation of Antofagasta; six days later, also the Bolivian population was informed of this event. The number of Bolivian regular soldiers was too small to confront Chile in a military conflict: this prompted Daza to form various new military units during the days that followed the declaration of war. He did so by using extensively the human resources coming from the National Guard and from the enlistment of volunteers. The response of the Bolivian people to Daza's general call to arms was patriotic and very enthusiastic. The dictator received complete popular support during the mobilization, because the occupation of Antofagasta and of such a rich region of the national territory was perceived as an outrage and as a betrayal by the Bolivians, who were absolutely convinced to have all the rights to reconquer it from the hated foreign invaders. In general terms, the war against Chile received great support from the middle classes and from the people living in the largest cities, while it was considered as an imposition by the Indios and by the poorest social classes of the country. Despite this, the

6 Greve-Moller P., Fernàndez-Cerda C., *Uniforms of the Pacific War 1879-1884*, Nottingham, 2010

Bolivian dictator was soon able to organize many new units, also thanks to an amnesty that was proclaimed to all the officers and soldiers who had opposed his rule until that date. In less than two months, by 14 April 1879, Daza had raised and superficially trained the new following units:

- Infantry Battalion "Tarija" (also known as "3rd Grenadiers of the Guard", formed in Tarija)

- Infantry Battalion "Olañeta" (also known as "2nd Cazadores of the Guard", formed in Sucre)

- Infantry Battalion "Victoria", 1st of La Paz

- Infantry Battalion "Paucarpata", 2nd of La Paz

- Infantry Battalion "Independencia", 3rd of La Paz

- Infantry Battalion "Oropesa", 1st of Cochabamba

- Infantry Battalion "Aroma", 1st of Cochabamba

- Infantry Battalion "Aroma", 2nd of Cochabamba

- Infantry Battalion "Viedma", 3rd of Cochabamba

- Infantry Battalion "Padilla", 4th of Cochabamba

- Infantry Battalion "Bustillos", 1st of Potosí

- Infantry Battalion "Ayacucho", 2nd of Potosí

- Infantry Battalion "Vengadores", 3rd of Potosí

- Infantry Battalion "Chorolque", 4th of Potosí

- Infantry Battalion "Dalence Carabineros", 1st of Oruro

- Infantry Battalion "Vengadores de Colquechaca" (formed in Colquechaca)

- Infantry Battalion "Columna Loa"

- Cavalry Squadron "Méndez", 2nd of Cuirassiers (formed in the department of Tarija)

- Cavalry Squadron "Junín", 3rd of Cuirassiers (formed in Cochabamba)

- Cavalry Squadron "Libertad", 4th of Cuirassiers (formed in the department of Cochabamba)

- Cavalry Squadron "Guías"

- Cavalry Squadron "Franco Tiradores"

- "Vanguard Division" (also known as "Bolivian Legion"), formed by the three cavalry squadrons "Rifleros del Norte" (aka "Murillo"), "Rifleros del Centro" (aka "Vanguardia") and "Rifleros del Sur" (aka "Libres del Sur")

With the addition of the military units listed above, the Bolivian Army deployed for the first campaign comprised 20 battalions of infantry, 10 squadrons of cavalry and 1 regiment of artillery [7]. Some of the new National Guard units had continued the numbering of the existing regular ones, for example the Battalion "Tarija" and the Battalion "Olañeta", which became respectively the "3rd Grenadiers of the Guard" and the "2nd Cazadores of the Guard". The same happened also with the cavalry squadrons "Méndez", "Junín" and "Libertad", which were numbered as the 2nd, 3rd and 4th Cuirassiers. In contrast with the 1st Squadron of Cuirassiers, however, the three new units were heavy cavalry in name only, having no helmets or cuirasses. The majority of the new infantry battalions adopted a progressive numbering based on the provenience of each unit, most of which were formed in the important cities of La Paz, Cochabamba and Potosí. It is interesting to note that two different battalions were known as the 1st of Cochabamba: the "Oropesa" and the "Aroma"; this was due to the fact that two units from Cochabamba were named "Aroma", so the first of these received the same number of the "Oropesa" Battalion. Similarly, to the three regular infantry battalions, the three National Guard ones formed in La Paz had red, yellow and green as distinctive colours: their uniforms were grey but had facings in the Bolivian national colours (red for the "Victoria", yellow for the "Paucarpata" and green for the "Independencia"). On paper, each Bolivian infantry battalion had to comprise four companies with 120 men each, bringing the total of each unit to 480 men. However, official establishments were rarely respected, and units generally had a number of soldiers that was inferior to the one officially prescribed (obviously there were some exceptions, like the "Colorados" Battalion that had 110 extra soldiers). Cavalry squadrons were formally structured on four companies and usually numbered between 80 and 150 men each.

The "Vanguard Division" or "Bolivian Legion" was a special volunteer cavalry unit that was formed to serve under direct command of Daza: it was made up of young volunteers coming from the well-educated elite and middle classes of the Bolivian society, who wished to serve their country with great patriotic spirit. Daza ordered its formation to have an elite force acting both as a sort of personal guard but also as a well-equipped independent cavalry force. The members of the "Bolivian Legion" were mounted and armed at their own expense. The three squadrons that made up the Legion usually fought as mounted infantry and not as proper cavalry: the volunteers rode into battle but dismounted to fight. In fact, the single units were named as "Rifleros", which means "riflemen". Daza paid special attention to the outfit of the "Vanguard Division", for example commissioning a special and elegant uniform made by French tailors for one of its squadrons (the "Rifleros del Sur") [8]. The new Bolivian military units raised by Daza included also two volunteer corps of exiles: the infantry battalion "Columna Loa" and the cavalry squadron "Franco Tiradores". The first was formed with Bolivians living in the Peruvian province of Tarapacá, most of whom worked in the local nitrate mines. Despite being a Bolivian unit, the "Columna Loa" was attached to the Peruvian forces during the first war campaign and followed them in all their movements. The "Franco Tiradores", instead, was a unit of middle-class volunteers coming from the Bolivian province of Antofagasta, which had just been occupied by the Chileans. Similarly, to the members of the "Bolivian Legion", they had to provide horses and equipment for themselves with no help from the government.

As a result of the severe defeat suffered at the Battle of San Francisco, on 19 November 1879, the Bolivian Army was completely reorganized. Much of its units, hastily assembled and sent to the front by Daza, had been destroyed in battle or had fled in disarray after being routed by the Chileans. The defeat, mainly caused by Daza's lack of military experience, had very important consequences also on the political situation of Bolivia: in December, Daza was deposed by a military coup and forced to go in exile in Europe. As

7 Estado Mayor General del Ejercito, *Historia del Ejercito de Chile*, Santiago, Chile, 1980-1983
8 Greve-Moller P., Fernàndez-Cerda C., *Uniformes de la Guerra del Pacífico 1879-1884*, Santiago, Chile, 2008

a result, a new government led by General Narciso Campero was formed, which soon started a general reorganization of the armed forces with the intention of continuing the war against Chile. Due to the very limited amount of available manpower, the number of infantry battalions had to be reduced from 20 to just 10, resulting in the following order of battle:

- 1st Line Infantry Battalion "Alianza" (ex "Colorados")

- 2nd Line Infantry Battalion "Sucre"

- 3rd Line Infantry Battalion "Loa" (ex Volunteer Battalion "Columna Loa")

- 4th Line Infantry Battalion "Aroma" (ex 1st National Guard Battalion of Cochabamba)

- 5th Line Infantry Battalion "Viedma" (ex 3rd National Guard Battalion of Cochabamba)

- 6th Line Infantry Battalion "Padilla" (ex 4th National Guard Battalion of Cochabamba)

- 7th Line Infantry Battalion "Tarija" (ex "3rd Grenadiers of the Guard")

- 8th Line Infantry Battalion "Chorolque" (ex 4th National Guard Battalion of Potosí)

- 9th Line Infantry Battalion "Grau"

- 10th Line Infantry Battalion "Columna Zapadores"

- Line Cavalry Squadron "Escolta", also known as "1st of Cuirassiers"

- Line Cavalry Squadron "Guías" (ex National Guard Squadron "Guías")

- Volunteer Cavalry Squadron "Murillo" (ex "Rifleros del Norte", 1st of the Bolivian Legion)

- Volunteer Cavalry Squadron "Vanguardia" (ex "Rifleros del Centro", 2nd of the Bolivian Legion)

- Volunteer Cavalry Squadron "Libres del Sur" (ex "Rifleros del Sur", 3rd of the Bolivian Legion)

- Artillery Regiment "Santa Cruz"

The "Colorados" Battalion, the unit that had been more strongly linked to Daza, was renamed "Alianza" and separated from its most fanatic members. The "Sucre" Battalion, instead, remained more or less the same. The "Illimani" Battalion, which had been completely destroyed on the battlefield, was substituted as the 3rd unit of the Bolivian infantry by the ex "Columna Loa" Battalion, a unit that had proved to be one of the best during the first campaign of the war. The battalions from four to eight were formed in a similar way, by re-naming National Guard units that had survived to the first campaign. All the remaining soldiers from the National Guard battalions that had been disbanded were grouped to form a new unit, the 9th Line Infantry Battalion "Grau". Regarding the "Columna Zapadores", we must point out that it was a special unit performing different kinds of military duties. In fact, despite being listed as an infantry battalion, its men performed also as sappers. It is highly probable that the Bolivians formed this unit following the example of Chile's elite "Zapadores de la Frontera"; in any case, the Bolivian sappers were organized in May 1880, shortly before the Battle of Tacna. One of the reasons behind the creation of this unit could be the Bolivian need for a corps of sappers that could build and maintain field fortifications, in view of the imminent and decisive pitched battle against the Chilean forces. The Bolivian cavalry was affected by the general reorganization of the army, but not as heavily as the infantry. While the "Cuirassiers" Squadron had remained practically intact, the "Hussars" Squadron had been completely annihilated by the Chileans during the cavalry clash at Pampa Germania (on 6 November 1879). The National Guard Squadron "Guías" was initially transformed into a line unit, but in April 1880 (while of garrison in Tacna) it was absorbed into the "Cuirassiers". The Bolivian Legion, one of Daza's creatures, was disbanded and its three squadrons continued to serve as individual units. The organization of the artillery remained the same.

Defeated for a second time in the Battle of Tacna (on 26 May 1880), the Bolivian forces retreated back to La Paz after having suffered very heavy human losses. In the following years of war, until the final surrender of Peru, the Bolivian armed forces played no active role in the military operations [9]. The war continued in the north, on the Peruvian territory, while the Bolivian region of Antofagasta remained in the hands of the Chileans. With a destroyed army and no hope of defeating the Chileans, the Bolivians remained passive for the rest of the conflict: they continued to give significant support to Peru in terms of military materials, but no Bolivian contingent

General Narciso Campero, President of Bolivia from January 1880 until 1884.

marched against the Chileans. In the period 1880-1884 the Bolivian Army was gradually rebuilt, with the introduction of many changes in its organization and the creation of various new units: in any case, these details are not important for our research, which is focused only on the military forces effectively involved into the War of the Pacific.

FORMATION AND COMPOSITION

Since its foundation, the Bolivian Army had a military academy for developing its officers: this had been created on 13 December 1825 by Simón Bolívar, but during the years that followed Bolivian independence it functioned only intermittently, mainly due to the many civil wars that eroded the Bolivian Army from the inside. In 1842 José Ballivián transferred the military academy to La Paz and chose as its director the Argentine officer Bartolomé Mitre, who later became President of Argentina and one of the most important figures in the military and political history of that country. In 1847, however, the institute was closed again. In 1859 the academy was re-established by President José Maria Linares, but it continued to work only until the ascendancy of Mariano Melgarejo in 1864. Until the fall of the latter in 1871, Bolivian officers were usually chosen according to their level of loyalty towards the military dictator. In 1872 the military academy was finally re-opened in a definitive way, under guidance of a veteran French officer. However, it did not train enough officers to change the general quality of the Bolivian officer corps in time for the war of 1879. By the outbreak of the War of the Pacific, most of the Bolivian officers had been appointed by Daza himself, thus being chosen for their loyalty to the dictator and not for their military preparation. The few expert ones, who had served under previous governments and who had not yet abandoned the country, were frequently obliged by Daza to serve as common soldiers and had no functions of command. In general, Bolivia's officers lacked the education and training to fight in a proper war, having no knowledge of modern weapons and tactics. Ineptitude and corruption were widespread, with the result that the totally

9 Sater, William F., *Andean Tragedy: Fighting the War of the Pacific 1879–1884*, University of Nebraska, 2007

politicized Bolivian officer corps was unable to train and lead its men properly. Additionally, the military of Bolivia lacked some of the basic institution of a modern army: for example, there were no general staff and corps of engineers. In the decades before the conflict, the Bolivian general staff had usually consisted of untrustworthy officers, who were detached to function as general staff in order to deprive them of command functions. As the military academy, also this important military institution functioned intermittently and was dominated by improvisation. At the outbreak of the new war, Daza tried to reorganize the Bolivian general staff, but apparently his actions had very little results. A real general staff was finally set up only after the general reorganization of the Bolivian armed forces in 1880. Regarding the engineer corps, we must point out that the Bolivian Army comprised a certain number of officers who were competent engineers; these, however, were very few and were not grouped into an official unit. In addition, until the very late creation of the "Columna Zapadores", they had no men at their disposal.

Bolivia had a conscription law as all the other South American countries of the time, but this was honoured only on paper. Before the war, recruiting operations usually proved to be quite difficult, since recruits were obtained thanks to the use of very harsh and frequently illegal methods (including violence). This system was deeply unjust, because only members of the lower social classes were enlisted: young members of the high and middle classes usually avoided service in the army thanks to corruption. Sometimes recruits who were formally exempted from military service were enlisted the same, in order to take the place of rich well-educated gentlemen. This situation changed with the outbreak of the war, when a general patriotic feeling led every social class of the country to contribute to the war effort. In general terms, the Bolivian common soldier had the same basic abilities of the Chilean or Peruvian equivalent, if not even superior ones[10]. Because of their usual harsh life-style, Bolivian rankers had the potential to perform very well on the field of battle, obviously if properly trained and led by their officers. The majority of the Bolivian recruits were Indios living in the largest cities or in the vast countryside of the Bolivian Plateau, who were accustomed to walk for miles in harsh terrain and had great resilience. They managed to survive with a very small quantity of toasted corn or cooked potatoes, being able to fight also after very long marches that reduced them naked and in need of everything. Many of the Bolivian Indios had not a very clear idea about the function of the war against Chile, but despite this they showed a great patriotic spirit. Those coming from the countryside were rarely able to understand a single word of the Spanish language spoken by their officers, with the result that there were significant difficulties in the transmission of orders. This was particularly true for the infantry, but not for the cavalry: the latter, in fact, was generally made up of well-to-do middle-class volunteers of Spanish descent. The bad military preparation of the Bolivian officers, however, prevented the recruits from transforming into a good fighting force.

Despite having bad leadership, poor equipment and obsolete weapons, the Bolivian infantrymen showed their courage in multiple occasions, receiving the admiration of their Chilean opponents. The "Colorados", for example, fought with extreme courage and great ability at the Battle of Tacna: they defeated four Chilean regiments ("Santiago", "Navales", "Esmeralda" and "Chillán") one after the other and then captured six guns from the enemy artillery. In the last phase of the battle, which resulted in a complete defeat for the Allies, they even resisted a strong Chilean cavalry charge by forming a solid defensive square. This outstanding performance of the "Colorados" was with no doubts the result of the excellent training that the unit had received since its creation, something that no other Bolivian unit fighting in the War of the Pacific had. In memory of the "Colorados" valour, May 26 (the day during which the Battle of Tacna was fought) is Bolivia's "Infantry Day". The cavalry had more or less the same problems of the infantry: the equipment and weaponry of the cavalrymen were generally more modern and adequate than those of the

---

10 Lòpez-Urrutia, Carlos, *La Guerra del Pacifico 1879-1884*, Madrid, 2003

infantrymen, but the deficiencies of the officer corps were exactly the same. Bolivian mounted units were generally affected by a chronic shortage of horses and men; the few available horses, in addition, were of very low quality. The situation was partly different for the units of volunteers that made up the "Bolivian Legion": coming from the rich middle classes of the country, these mounted riflemen usually had good horses and modern weapons. The Bolivian artillery was with no doubts the branch of service with the most serious problems: at the beginning of the war it had very few men and guns; the former lacked any kind of specific training, while the latter were usually old pieces. There were no decent horses to transport the guns on the field of battle and the few artillery officers lacked the technical skills needed to fire them accurately. In practice, the small artillery corps deployed by Bolivia during the first two war campaigns was not even worth mentioning. New modern guns were bought after 1880, but not in time to be employed against the Chileans.

WEAPONS

At the beginning of the war, the three regular infantry battalions of the Bolivian Army were armed with different weapons: the elite "Colorados" and the "Illimani" Battalion were armed with the excellent 11mm M1871 Remington rolling-block rifle, while the "Sucre" Battalion carried the so-called "Castañon" rifles[11]. The latter were nothing else than M1866 Chassepot paper-cartridge rifles that had been modified in Peru to take the same 11mm brass cartridge of the Comblain rifle. The "Colorados" had been the first Bolivian unit to receive Remington rifles: thanks to this superior weapon, they were able to maintain a leading role inside the Bolivian military forces. In total, the Bolivians had received 1,000 "Castañon" rifles from Peru: these were given back to the Peruvians once a new stock of Remington's arrived from the USA. In fact, in March 1879, the Bolivian military forces received 1,500 new M1871 Remington's, which replaced the Peruvian rifles as main weapon of the "Sucre" Battalion. As a result, all the Bolivian regular battalions came to be armed with the same infantry weapon; in total, considering also the 1,500 ones possessed before the outbreak of the hostilities (bought in 1878), the Bolivian Army employed 3,000 M1871 Remington's. The Bolivian Remington's were all of the same model but could have two different manufactures: the original 1,500 already possessed before the war had been produced in Spain, while the new 1,500 bought in 1879 were produced in the USA. However, these were too few to equip all the new National Guard infantry battalions that were formed following Daza's general mobilization.

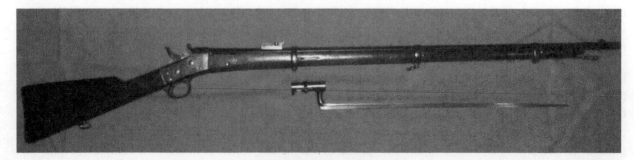

M1871 Remington

Apparently, the new battalions received a very small number of Remington rifles, because the government gave priority to the equipment of the three regular battalions. Despite this, we know for sure that the battalions "Aroma" (1st of Cochabamba) and "Tarija" were equipped with Remington rifles. At least for the Battalion "Aroma", there is an historical reason behind the issue of Remington rifles to the unit: this

11 Greve-Moller P., Fernàndez-Cerda C., *Uniforms of the Pacific War 1879-1884*, Nottingham, 2010

National Guard battalion, in fact, was considered as the best among the new National Guard units formed in 1879. It was an elite infantry corps: in practical terms, it was created and considered as the National Guard equivalent of the regular "Colorados". Their affiliation to Daza's praetorians was apparent in the use of the same weapons, but also because they wore a red uniform that was very similar to that of the 1st Line Infantry Battalion. For the latter reason, the "Aroma" Battalion from Cochabamba had the nickname of "Coloraditos" (which means "Little Reds"). However, the majority of the new National Guard infantry battalions were not as lucky as the "Coloraditos" or "Tarija": they had been hastily assembled and trained by Daza, thus receiving old and inadequate weaponry. To equip these soldiers, the Bolivian government employed a bewildering variety of weapons: during the first war campaign, the most popular infantry weapons of the National Guard units were old percussion muskets and even older flintlock ones. In this situation of emergency, every kind of weaponry that was available in military stores was given to soldiers. The "Columna Loa", for example, was armed with Peruvian "Castañon" rifles, but many other kinds of rifles were also in use: the most popular one, with no doubts, was the British M1866 Snider-Enfield rifle (the breech-loading conversion of the Pattern 1853 Enfield). In addition to this, the Bolivian infantrymen employed also Comblain and Peabody-Martini rifles, which were usually obtained from Peru. Comblain rifles captured from the Chileans were obviously re-used. As the conflict progressed, with the military preparations for the second war campaign, the Bolivians received increasingly high numbers of weapons from their Peruvian allies: these consisted of "Castañon", Peabody-Martini and Comblain rifles (all infantry weapons that were largely employed by the Peruvian Army).

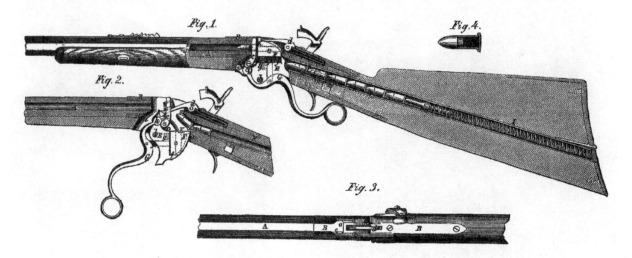

The mechanism of the US M1860 Spencer carbine, employed by the Bolivian cavalry.

If the situation of the infantry weapons was quite confused, this was particularly true also for those employed by the cavalry, since there were no standard models and many cavalry units were composed of volunteers who had to provide weapons and equipment for themselves at their own expense[12]. Of the two regular squadrons existing before the war, only the 1st Hussars had modern weaponry, because the 1st of Cuirassiers was equipped only with French-made sabres and lances. Having a purely ceremonial function, Daza's cuirassiers did not need modern weapons; their lances, which were not carried by officers, also had no practical function. Regarding the 1st Hussars, we must point out that the cavalrymen from this unit were equipped quite well, with French-made sabres and M1865 Spencer carbines bought from the USA. Later in the war, as a result of the increasing number of weapons being supplied by Peru, the

12 Lòpez-Urrutia, Carlos, *La Guerra del Pacifico 1879-1884*, Madrid, 2003

31

Bolivian hussars replaced their Spencer carbines with M1871 Remington ones. Regarding the weaponry of the three National Guard cuirassier squadrons formed by Daza, the available information is quite detailed: the "Méndez" and "Libertad" squadrons were armed with M1871 Remington cavalry carbines and sabres, while the cavalrymen of the "Junín" Squadron were equipped as lancers (with cavalry lances, sabres and M1871 Remington carbines). As for the regular cuirassiers, officers of this unit had no lances and replaced carbines with different kinds of revolvers. The "Guías" Squadron used M1871 Remington and M1860 Spencer cavalry carbines. The "Franco Tiradores", instead, had M1871 Remington and M1877 Martini-Henry cavalry carbines. Both units apparently carried no sabres. Regarding the weapons employed by the three squadrons that made up the "Bolivian Legion", these were generally equipped with M1871 Remington carbines, received directly from Daza. In addition to these, they used also a certain number of M1860

Gatling machine gun, employed by all the armies involved in the conflict.

Spencer and M1866 or M1873 Winchester carbines. As for the infantry ones, Bolivian cavalry officers were armed with privately-purchased revolvers and sabres; both of these were made in France, with Lefaucheux revolvers being quite popular.

For what regards artillery, as we previously said this was the branch of the Bolivian Army that had the most serious problems in terms of weaponry and equipment. At the beginning of the war, the Bolivian artillery comprised 10 to 15 old smoothbore guns and four much modern rifled pieces (bought in 1872). The latter were two 12-pdr muzzle-loading Blakely guns and two La Hitte field pieces. In addition, the Artillery Regiment "Santa Cruz" also had four Gatling machine guns (which formed an autonomous and mobile detachment of light artillery). The few artillerymen were armed with the same M1871 Remington carbines of the cavalry. With the progression of the hostilities, it became soon clear to the Bolivian authorities that four modern guns were too few to confront the larger and better equipped Chilean artillery. In 1879 six 6cm Krupp mountain guns were bought, bringing the total of modern Bolivian artillery pieces to 10. Following the defeat of 1880, the Bolivian artillery was totally re-founded, with the purchase of more Krupp guns and the formation of the 2nd Artillery Regiment "Bolívar". In 1881, thanks to shipments coming from Panama, other six 6cm Krupp mountain guns were bought; in 1883, two batteries with six 87mm Krupp field guns were also bought. One of the latter field batteries was then given to Peru in October 1883, in exchange for a battery of Krupp mountain guns that had been bought by the Peruvians and that was transiting on the Bolivian territory.

UNIFORMS

At the time of the War of the Pacific Bolivian uniforms were not following any official dress regulation but had a series of common features that made all of them quite similar. In contrast with Chile and Peru, Bolivia did not have a General Supply Corps (it had been created in 1859 but was dismantled as soon as the war began)[13]: the manufacture of uniforms was given to women of all social classes living in various areas of the country, who very often had quite little tailoring experience. In addition, the producers of these craft uniforms were sometimes supplied by the government with fabrics that were not appropriate to the local climate and terrain of Bolivia. As a result, many of the Bolivian uniforms could not endure the hardships of a military campaign. Cloth was normally imported via Peru and not directly from the Bolivian ports; for this reason, when Daza expanded his army for war, he was obliged to seize all existing wool in the country (locally known as "bayeta"). In general terms, Bolivian military dress was heavily influenced by the French military fashions of the previous decades: this was mainly due to the fact that Daza had a fatal fascination for Napoleon III's Imperial Army, which was apparent in the cut of the uniforms that was chosen for the Bolivian Army. Bolivian uniforms had been influenced by French models since the 1830s, starting with the dress regulations that were promulgated by President Andrés de Santa Cruz (the future creator of the Peru-Bolivian Confederation). The French influence was maintained during the presidency of José Ballivián (1841–47), albeit being mitigated by the adoption of Bolivian national colours as main colours for the production of uniforms. Under Mariano Melgarejo, Bolivian uniforms started to copy the military dress of Napoleon III's Army, as part of a general South American trend that saw the adoption of French military fashions in various countries of that continent. It was under Melgarejo, for example, that the newly-formed escort Regiment of Cuirassiers adopted a parade dress very similar to that worn by Napoleon III's "Cent-Gardes" Squadron. This new trend continued also during the turbulent years that followed Melgarejo's fall, being brought to its highest point under Daza's rule. The latter was probably one of the most despotic rulers ever seen in South America, being under many aspects one of the last great "caudillos"

13 Greve-Moller P., Fernàndez-Cerda C., *Uniforms of the Pacific War 1879-1884*, Nottingham, 2010

of that continent. His small and personal army was perfectly dressed, but in practice it was an army only on paper. When the Bolivian armed forces were reorganized in 1876, following Daza's ascendancy to power, they received new uniforms in perfect French style. Many of the new pieces of clothing were surplus from France, which had belonged to the Imperial Army of Napoleon III that had been disbanded after the war of 1870 against Prussia. As a result, Daza's "Colorados" received the massive bearskins of Napoleon III's Grenadiers of the Guard, while the Bolivian cuirassiers were equipped with surplus helmets and cuirasses of the French "Cent-gardes" Squadron. The new infantry uniforms introduced by Daza consisted of shakos, double-breasted tunics and very large trousers, of clear French cut. However, when the war broke out in 1879, the three regular battalions already in existence had to abandon their ornate uniforms in La Paz and adopt simpler ones with kepis, short jackets and normal trousers.

When Daza had to recruit new units in view of the military confrontation with Chile, these had to be dressed in what was available, leading to the production of many improvised uniforms. As the war progressed, these uniforms began to deteriorate, and Bolivian soldiers started to experience very serious problems regarding dress provisions: in the last months of the second campaign they were lucky to have a single uniform item, like a jacket or a kepi. To face this problem, the army had to requisition clothing material from various warehouses, located in the main Bolivian cities. In general terms, the uniforms of the new National Guard infantry battalions were exact copies of the basic dress worn by the regular infantry; the new cavalry squadrons, instead, had very simple uniforms. Some units, like the "Franco Tiradores", did not have uniforms at all. The basic dress of the Bolivian infantryman included the following standard elements: kepi (frequently having a white protective cover or a white cover for the neck), jacket (with collar, cuffs and frontal piping in the unit's facing colour), trousers and sandals. The main colour and the facing colour of the jacket were usually taken from the Bolivian national flag. Two main features made Bolivian uniforms very easy to recognize: the first was the profusion of decorative buttons on the sleeves of the jacket, while the second were the enormously deep and slanting cuffs (usually piped with a contrasting colour). Rank was shown by inverted "chevrons", which were red for corporals and yellow for sergeants. The bullhide sandals (known as "ojotas") were usually preferred to black leather shoes during campaign, because they were very comfortable for long marches. For protection of the lower part of the leg, protectors of white coarse cloth were sewn on to the roll up trousers, allowing air to circulate but at the same time protecting the soldiers' feet from the sun. Personal equipment was usually reduced to a minimum: leather bag, metal canteen and black leather waist belt holding a couple of cartridge pouches. The leather bags were trimmed with multicoloured wool, in the fashion of the Indios living on the Bolivian Andes. For protection against enemy bayonets and a much more comfortable wearing of the waist belt, Bolivian infantrymen usually carried a striped "poncho" wrapped around the waist. This was also a perfect protection against cold during nights in the Desert of Atacama. As the war progressed, leather cartridge pouches gradually deteriorated due to the dry and salty environmental conditions in which the conflict was fought: as a result, they were replaced by new canvas cartridge belts made by the same soldiers (named "cananas") or by long ammunition bags (also made of canvas and known as "talegas").

Officers: In contrast from the common soldiers, who were dressed in jackets in the distinctive colours of each unit, Bolivian infantry and artillery officers were all dressed in simple dark blue uniforms, which made them very easy to recognize[14]. Only the few high officers who had important functions of command were not dressed in this way, instead having privately-purchased ornate parade uniforms with cocked hats and long-tailed coatees. This kind of parade dress was used in a series of different patterns, according to the personal taste of each individual, but all quite similar among them because being inspired by the parade

14 Greve-Moller P., Fernàndez-Cerda C., *Uniformes de la Guerra del Pacifico 1879-1884*, Santiago, Chile, 2008

34

uniforms of Napoleon III and of his general staff. The same Daza was usually dressed in this fashion, with black bicorn hat having white ostrich-feather plumage. The long-tailed coatee was dark blue and had gold oakleaf embroidery on collar, cuffs and frontal plastron. Golden epaulettes were usually worn, together with dark blue or white trousers (the former normally had golden side stripes). A tricolour sash in Bolivia's national colours was frequently worn on the right shoulder, to complete this elegant outfit.

The service uniform was instead much simpler and more practical for use on campaign. It could be of two main different patterns: single-breasted or double-breasted. The single-breasted one consisted of a dark blue frock coat of French cut, having red piping to collar, front and cuffs (which were of the usual Bolivian slanting pattern and were closed by a profusion of small buttons). Epaulettes were rarely worn on this uniform, usually being substituted by golden epaulet-loops. Rank was indicated by golden inverted rank "chevrons" on the cuffs, just above the red piping. The uniform was completed by large dark blue trousers having broad golden side stripes. Apparently, this uniform was quite popular before the war, being gradually replaced by the simpler double-breasted one as the conflict progressed. The latter was much more modern than the one described above: dark blue double-breasted tunic, having golden epaulet-loops on the shoulders and inverted rank "chevrons" on the sleeves. No piping and no buttons on the sleeves. Both versions of the Bolivian infantry and artillery officers' uniform could bear a golden device on the collar: respectively, this was a "chasseur" horn or a flaming grenade. Apparently, these devices were usually worn by the officers coming from the units that already existed before the war. The double-breasted uniform was completed by dark blue trousers of normal cut having red side stripes.

In regard to the headgear, Bolivian officers could wear either the shako or the kepi: generally speaking, the shako was more popular in the first phase of the war and was usually worn in combination with the single-breasted frock coat. The kepi, more modern and practical than the shako, started to be commonly used after the first months of campaign, usually having a white cover for protection of the neck and being worn together with the double-breasted dark blue tunic. The shako was dark blue, with golden top band and piping: the latter was located on the sides and on the bottom band of the shako, showing rank of the officer; it corresponded to the number of inverted "chevrons" on the sleeves (a captain, for example, had three inverted "chevrons" on the sleeves and triple piping on the sides and bottom band of the shako). In addition, the shako had a pompom and a cockade in the national colours of Bolivia. Sometimes it also bore a golden unit device, like a "chasseur" horn or a flaming grenade. The kepi, instead, was very simple: entirely dark blue and with golden rank piping. Unit devices were sometimes worn on it, but less frequently than on shakos. The personal equipment of Bolivian officers was usually reduced to a minimum, consisting of a simple black leather waist belt which buckle could be decorated with the Bolivian coat-of-arms. Leather pouches for documents and maps were also quite common. On campaign, all the Bolivian officers were dressed in dark blue, with the exception of those who carried the ensigns of their unit: these, in fact, were dressed exactly like the rankers. The only difference that made them recognizable as officers was the use of a longer single-breasted tunic instead of the rankers' short jacket; this peculiar item of dress was in the distinctive colour of the unit but had additional piping on each side of the front.

"Colorados" Battalion (later "Alianza" Battalion): During the period 1876-1879, the battalion wore a very extravagant parade uniform, which was issued by Daza soon after his ascendancy to power. The "Colorados" were not the only Bolivian infantry unit to have this kind of uniform but were the only to wear a massive bearskin as a sign of their elite status and of their special functions as "praetorians" of Daza. The dictator, in fact, decided to give to his personal unit a French-style uniform that could reflect the battalion's denomination of "Grenadiers of the Guard". As usual, the model after which this dress was patterned was found in the Imperial Guard of Napoleon III. As we previously said, the infantry uniforms issued in 1876 by Daza included a double-breasted tunic: for the "Colorados" this was red, with black collar, frontal piping and slanting cuffs. The cuffs were piped in white and had many small buttons[15]. On each side of the collar there was a decorative brass flaming grenade, the conventional device of the grenadiers. As for the other two battalions, the trousers were extremely large, having the same cut of those worn by the contemporary French Zouaves. They were white and had black side stripes. Except for colours, this was the same dress worn by the "Sucre" and "Illimani" battalions during the period 1876-1879: the "Sucre" had yellow tunics with red collar, frontal piping and cuffs, while the "Illimani" had green tunics with black collar, frontal piping and cuffs. The "Sucre" Battalion had the same flaming grenades of the "Colorados", while the "Illimani" Battalion had brass "chasseur" horns on the collar (being considered as a unit of light infantry). The uniform of the "Colorados", however, was made peculiar by the exclusive use of a massive grenadier bearskin; the other two battalions, in fact, had a different and less extravagant headgear consisting of a shako with plume in the national colours, brass frontal plate, decorative cords and flounders. The bearskins of the "Colorados" were bought by Daza from the famous Godillot firm of Paris, being surplus items of the disbanded French Imperial Guard. Once dispatched to Bolivia, the bearskins of the Imperial Guard Grenadiers were modified in order to have a more Bolivian appearance. The brass frontal plate was painted with three bands in the Bolivian national colours and a plume with the same colours was added to the right side of the headgear. Golden cords and flounders, together with a large flaming grenade located above the frontal plate, completed the new rich decorations of the bearskin. In addition, the original chinstrap was covered with fur, in order to resemble a beard: this could seem quite strange, but according to Daza a long beard was both a symbol of masculinity and a proper feature of grenadiers. All the belt equipment was white and the buckle of waist belt bore the number of the unit between two laurel branches.

The new dress given to the battalion in 1879 was a perfect example of the standard Bolivian infantry uniform, which was used by all battalions during the war: black kepi with green bottom band and yellow piping, having brass flaming grenade on the front and national cockade. Pompom in national colours, black leather visor and chinstrap. Red jacket with black collar, slanting cuffs and frontal piping. White piping to the cuffs, brass flaming grenades on the collar. White trousers with black side stripes. Differentiating it from the other two regular battalions, the "Colorados" had two lines of additional black piping on each side of the jacket (which passed on the shoulders and continued also on the back). The "Colorados" Battalion, as well as the "Sucre" and "Illimani" ones, was easily recognizable thanks to the use of a white scarf with three decorative horizontal stripes (known as "bufanda"). These scarves were not employed by the new National Guard units formed after the declaration of war, so they soon became a distinctive feature of the original regular battalions. According to a contemporary Chilean chronicler, the red cloth of the "Colorados" uniforms was of excellent quality, having been bought by Daza in 1876 from the French merchant Guillot, who was established in La Paz. Apparently, this red cloth was surplus one coming from France, having been formerly used to produce the uniforms of the Imperial Guard. The adoption of the new name ("Alianza") did not change any detail of the unit's uniform.

"Sucre" Battalion: red kepi with green bottom band and yellow piping, having brass flaming grenade on the front and national cockade. Pompom in national colours, black leather visor and chinstrap. Yellow jacket with red collar, slanting cuffs and frontal piping. White piping to the cuffs and white trousers with red side stripes. The uniform remained the same also for the second campaign[16].

---

15 Fernandez-Asturizaga, Augusto, *Uniformes Militares Bolivianos 1827-1988*, La Paz, Bolivia, 1991
16 Greve-Moller P., Fernàndez-Cerda C., *Uniforms of the Pacific War 1879-1884*, Nottingham, 2010

Soldier of the "Sucre" Battalion; note the protectors of coarse cloth and bullhide sandals.

"Illimani" Battalion: red kepi with green bottom band and yellow piping, having brass "chasseur" horn on the front and national cockade. Pompom in national colours, black leather visor and chinstrap. Green jacket with red collar, slanting cuffs and frontal piping. White piping to the cuffs and white trousers with black side stripes. This unit used also trousers with different colours, being dark blue with red side stripes.

"Tarija" Battalion: white kepi with red bottom band and pompom in national colours, black leather visor and chinstrap. White jacket with red collar, slanting cuffs and frontal piping. White trousers with red side stripes. This unit was later transformed into the 7th Battalion of the Line, thus adopting this new uniform for the second campaign: white kepi with green bottom band and piping, black leather visor and chinstrap. White jacket with green collar, slanting cuffs and frontal piping. White trousers with green side stripes.

"Victoria" Battalion: grey kepi with red piping, black leather visor and chinstrap. Grey jacket with red collar, slanting cuffs and frontal piping. Grey trousers with red side stripes.

"Paucarpata" Battalion: grey kepi with yellow piping, black leather visor and chinstrap. Grey jacket with yellow collar, slanting cuffs and frontal piping. Grey trousers with yellow side stripes.

"Independencia" Battalion: grey kepi with green piping, black leather visor and chinstrap. Grey jacket with green collar, slanting cuffs and frontal piping. Grey trousers with green side stripes.

"Aroma" Battalion, 1st of Cochabamba: the soldiers of this unit were known as "Coloraditos", because they had exactly the same red uniform of Daza's "Colorados". For this reason, on various occasions, the Chileans confused them with the regular "Grenadiers of the Guard". The only difference between the uniform of this battalion and that of the "Colorados" was in the trousers: those of the regular unit were white with black side stripe, while those of the "Aroma" Battalion were grey with red side stripe. In addition, the "Aroma" did not have the peculiar white scarf with three red horizontal stripes of the regulars. The uniform remained the same also for the second campaign.

"Viedma" Battalion: red kepi with green bottom band and piping, black leather visor and chinstrap. Green jacket with red collar, slanting cuffs and frontal piping. Grey trousers with red side stripes. The uniform remained the same also for the second campaign.

"Padilla" Battalion: red kepi with green bottom band and yellow piping, having pompom in national colours, black leather visor and chinstrap. Green jacket with black collar, slanting cuffs and frontal piping. Grey trousers with black side stripes. The uniform remained the same for the second campaign.

"Chorolque" Battalion: dark blue kepi with red top band and pompom in national colours, black leather visor and chinstrap. Dark blue jacket with red collar, slanting cuffs and frontal piping. White trousers with red side stripes. The uniform remained the same also for the second campaign.

"Columna Loa" Battalion: during the first campaign, this unit used two different uniforms. The first of these was a provisional one, produced with a certain degree of improvisation due to the Chilean blockade of the Peruvian port of Iquique. It consisted of red kepi with dark blue bottom band and yellow piping, black leather visor and chinstrap. Dark blue blouse with white vertical stripes, red collar, slanting cuffs and frontal piping. Dark blue trousers with red side stripes. As clear from this description, this first uniform was nothing else than the working dress used by Bolivian workers in the Peruvian mines, with the addition of some military elements to the striped blouse. With the progression of the hostilities, however, the

"Columna Loa" Battalion was expanded (from two to four companies) and received a proper uniform like all the other Bolivian infantry battalions[17]: red kepi with dark blue bottom band and yellow piping, black leather visor and chinstrap. Dark blue jacket with red collar, slanting cuffs and frontal piping. Red trousers with dark blue side stripes. With the reorganization of the Bolivian Army for the second war campaign, the Battalion "Columna Loa" was renamed "Loa" and took the place of the "Illimani" Battalion as 3rd of the Line (the "Illimani" had been completely destroyed by the Chileans). As a result of this change of status, the battalion changed for the third time its uniform, adopting that previously worn by the "Illimani" regular battalion but continuing to wear the same old kepi. The resulting new uniform was as follows: red kepi with dark blue bottom band and yellow piping, black leather visor and chinstrap. Green jacket with red collar, slanting cuffs and frontal piping. Dark blue trousers with red side stripes.

"Grau" Battalion: red kepi with green bottom band and yellow piping, having national cockade on the front and pompom in national colours, black leather visor and chinstrap. White jacket with red collar, slanting cuffs and frontal piping. Grey trousers with red side stripes.

Unfortunately, we have no details about the uniforms used by the following infantry battalions: "Olañeta", "Oropesa", "Aroma" (2nd of Cochabamba), "Bustillos", "Ayacucho", "Vengadores", "Dalence Carabineros", "Vengadores de Colquechaca" and "Columna Zapadores". As you can note, with the exception of the "Columna Zapadores", these are all units that were formed for the first campaign and were completely destroyed during it.

"Bolívar" Squadron: the uniform of the Bolivian "1st Hussars" was quite similar to that of the Chilean

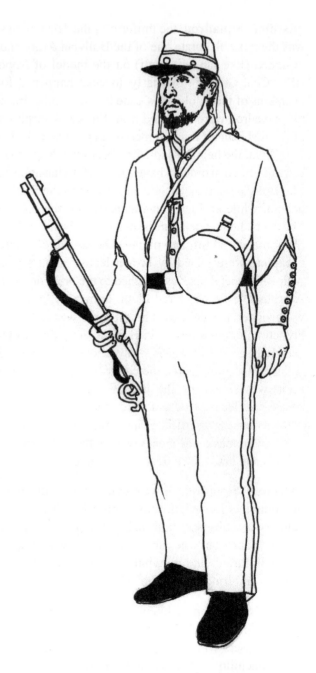

Soldier of the "Columna Loa" Battalion, wearing this unit's second uniform. Drawing by Benedetto Esposito.

"Granaderos a Caballo", thus leading to some confusion on the field of battle. It consisted of red kepi with dark blue bottom band and piping, black leather visor and chinstrap. The kepi had a brass device on the front (an Inca Sun) and was frequently worn together with a white protective cover for the neck. Dark blue jacket with red piping to collar, slanting cuffs and front. Red trousers with dark blue side stripes.

---

17 Greve-Moller P., Fernàndez-Cerda C., *Uniforms of the Pacific War 1879-1884*, Nottingham, 2010

"Escolta" Squadron: the uniform of the "1st Cuirassiers" was the most elaborate one of the Bolivian Army and was designed (like the unit itself) on the model of Napoleon III's "Cent-Gardes". Similarly, to what happened for the bearskins of the "Colorados", the helmets and cuirasses of this squadron were imported from France as surplus items of the disbanded French Imperial Guard. Once dispatched to Bolivia, the helmets and cuirasses of the "Cent-Gardes" were modified in order to have a more Bolivian appearance. The Bolivian national shield was added to the front of the helmet, while an Inca Sun was added on the breastplate. The steel helmet had brass crest, visor and chinscales, black mane, red tuft and plume. The steel breastplate and backplate were joined by brown leather shoulder straps, with white metal buckles attached to the brass decorations. A protective lining of red cloth, known as "fraise", was worn under the cuirass. The uniform was produced by French tailors established in Bolivia, according to Daza's personal taste. It consisted of a yellow jacket with green collar and slanting cuffs, the collar being piped in yellow. Rank was shown by the use of golden epaulettes and contre-epaulettes. Trousers were made of light grey cloth with darker grey vertical stripes; they also had red side-stripes. Pennons of the lances were in the Bolivian national colours and had golden decorative fringes.

"Méndez" Squadron: as we previously said, the new units of cuirassiers formed after the outbreak of the war had no helmets or cuirasses, thus being equipped as any other cavalry squadron. The simple uniform of this squadron was as follows: entirely white kepi and jacket, dark blue trousers and fringed "poncho" in the local fashion[18].

"Junín" Squadron: red kepi with green bottom band and yellow piping. Black jacket with dark blue slanting cuffs, black trousers with three dark blue side stripes. Entirely red "ponchillos" (smaller and shorter "ponchos", with no fringes). Pennons of the lances were in the Bolivian national colours.

Trooper of the Line Cavalry Squadron "Bolívar", also known as "1st of Hussars". Drawing by Benedetto Esposito.

"Libertad" Squadron: unfortunately, no details of the uniform are known.

"Guías" Squadron: green kepi with red bottom band and yellow piping. Red double-breasted jacket with green collar, slanting cuffs and lapels (usually worn partially open). White trousers with three red side stripes.

---

18 Fernandez-Asturizaga, Augusto, *Uniformes Militares Bolivianos 1827-1988*, La Paz, Bolivia, 1991

Bolivian mounted volunteers, dressed with civilian clothes like the "Franco Tiradores".

"Franco Tiradores" Squadron: the young volunteers of this unit had no uniforms, being dressed in their civilian clothes.

"Rifleros del Norte" Squadron: as the other two squadrons that made up the "Bolivian Legion", this unit had two different uniforms. The first one consisted of black kepi with green top band and piping, black jacket with green collar, slanting cuffs and piping to the front and bottom edges, having green frogging on the front. Black trousers with three green side stripes. The second uniform was much simpler: entirely black kepi and jacket, having black piping and frogging. Entirely black trousers.

"Rifleros del Centro" Squadron: the first uniform consisted of entirely black kepi, grey jacket with red collar, slanting cuffs and piping to the front and bottom edges, having red frogging on the front. Black trousers with three red side stripes. The second uniform was exactly the same as worn by the "Rifleros del Norte": entirely black kepi and jacket, having black piping and frogging. Entirely black trousers.

"Rifleros del Sur" Squadron: the first uniform of this squadron was particularly elegant, because it was commissioned by the same Daza to some French tailors who were established in Bolivia[19]. It consisted of dark blue kepi with red bottom band and piping, dark blue jacket with red collar, round cuffs and piping to the front and bottom edges. In addition, the jacket was decorated on the front with three rows of buttons,

19 Greve-Moller P., Fernàndez-Cerda C., *Uniforms of the Pacific War 1879-1884*, Nottingham, 2010

41

Trooper of the "Rifleros del Centro" Squadron, wearing this unit's first uniform. Drawing by Benedetto Esposito.

The "Rifleros del Sur" Squadron; rankers are wearing this unit's second uniform.

which were set on red bands. The back of the jacket was trimmed with red lace. The upper sleeves had three red inverted "chevrons", which were purely decorative (they were not used to show rank). The outfit was completed by dark blue trousers with three red side stripes. As for the other two squadrons, the second uniform was simpler than the original one: entirely red kepi, grey jacket with red collar, slanting cuffs and piping to the front. White trousers with three red side stripes.

"Santa Cruz" Regiment: white kepi with red bottom band, black visor and chinstrap. White jacket with red collar and pointed cuffs, brass buttons. White trousers with red double side-stripe.

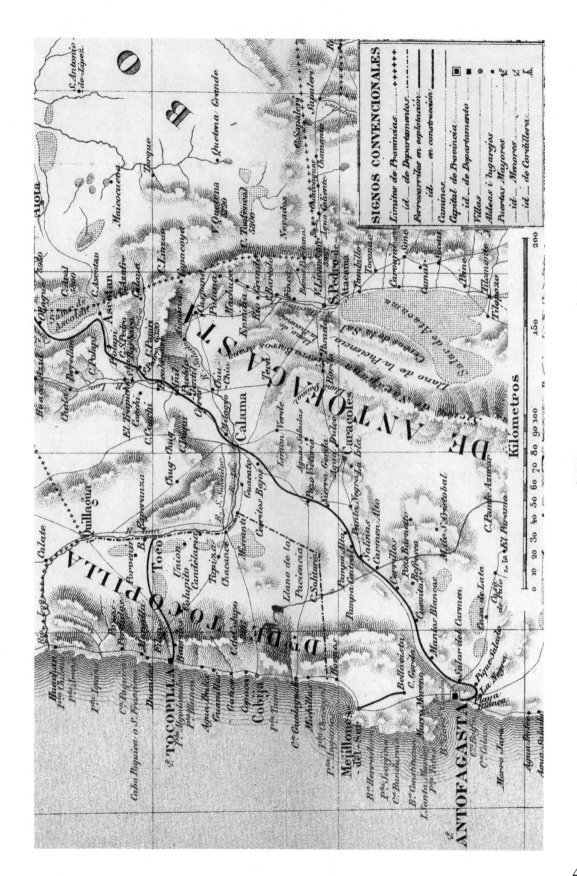

Mariano Ignacio Prado Ochoa, President of Peru during 1876-1879.

THE PERUVIAN ARMY

ORGANIZATION

The outbreak of the War of the Pacific found the Peruvian Army in a state of complete unpreparedness, similarly to what happened to the Bolivian military forces. In general terms the Peruvian Army had many problems in common with the Bolivian one, but its structure was more solid, and its officers were more experienced than the relative Bolivian counterparts. In any case, as with Daza's army, the number of regular soldiers was too small to confront Chile in a large-scale conflict, while the ratio between the number of officers and rankers was absolutely ridiculous as in the Bolivian Army[20]. In total, the Peruvian Army of 1879 deployed 6,160 men, very little if compared with the large population of the country; 2,679 of these were officers on active service or in the reserve, including 25 generals – approximately 43% rather than the norm of around 15%. In contrast to Bolivia, however, this general state of military unpreparedness was the result of a failed reformation attempt, initiated by Lima's government in 1873. In that year the Peruvian authorities had finally decided to start a complete reorganization of their armed forces, with the clear ambition of transforming them into a professional army within a few years. According to these plans, the core of the new military formations that were to be created had to be the NCOs who were in the process of being trained in the newly-established "Escuela de Clases" (the academy for sergeants and corporals, active since 1873). The outbreak of the war with Chile, however, prevented the Peruvians from completing their difficult military reforms, with the result that the organization of the army had to be reverted to the situation of 1872, in order to face the emergency. It is important to note, however, that the reformation process was decisively slowed down by economic and political difficulties: similarly, to what happened in other South American armies, Peru's officer corps became bloated as the result of the officers' involvement in politics and of their widespread corruption. Since independence from Spain, the political history of Peru had been characterised by continuous military coups and the army had played a fundamental role in the institutional life of the country. From the beginning, Peruvian politicians were divided into two large categories: those who supported military governments (the majority of whom were officers themselves) and those who were in favour of civilian governments. To complicate the situation, however, these two factions were additionally divided into smaller groups. Generally speaking, the military was always divided between officers who currently held power and those who wished to take the place of the former as soon as possible. Bearing in mind all these factors, it is easy to understand why the Peruvian Army of 1879 included just eight battalions of infantry, three regiments of cavalry and two regiments of artillery:

- 1st Line Infantry Battalion "Pichincha"

- 2nd Line Infantry Battalion "Zepita"

---

20 Sater, William F., *Andean Tragedy: Fighting the War of the Pacific 1879–1884*, University of Nebraska, 2007

- 3rd Line Infantry Battalion "Ayacucho"

- 4th Line Infantry Battalion "Callao"

- 5th Line Infantry Battalion "Cazadores del Cuzco"

- 6th Line Infantry Battalion "Cazadores de Puno"

- 7th Line Infantry Battalion "Cazadores de la Guardia"

- 8th Line Infantry Battalion "Lima"

- 1st Line Cavalry Regiment "Húsares de Junín"

- 2nd Line Cavalry Regiment "Lanceros de Torata"

- 3rd Line Cavalry Regiment "Guías"

- 1st Artillery Regiment "2 de Mayo" (field artillery)

- 2nd Artillery Regiment (garrison artillery)

These little forces were dispersed in various garrisons, located across the large territory of Peru. On paper, each Peruvian infantry battalion was to number 600 men, divided into 12 companies of 50 men each. Official establishments, however, were rarely reached and thus the average pre-war Peruvian battalions usually numbered around 500 soldiers each. The three cavalry units were regiments with two squadrons and numbered 260 men each. The two regiments of artillery numbered 500 men each, so more or less had the same establishment of an infantry battalion. As we have indicated in the previous order of battle, just the first artillery regiment (which had a name) was a field unit, while the second was a regiment of garrison artillery: its primary function was to manage the large number of fortress guns that were located in Lima or in Callao (the strategic port of the Peruvian capital). The 500 men of the garrison artillery were deployed in six defensive batteries and six forts of different dimensions. When Chile declared war on 5 April 1879, the Peruvians had to expand their military forces as soon as possible: the only way to do this was to rely heavily on the volunteers of the National Guard, which could mobilize up to 65,000 able-bodied men. In general terms, the organization and recruiting systems of the Peruvian National Guard were better than those of the Bolivian one but were largely inferior if compared with those of the Chilean counterpart. The following National Guard units were formed and mobilized for the first war campaign of 1879:

- Infantry Battalion "Ayacucho"

- Infantry Battalion "Cazadores de Tarapacá"

- Infantry Battalion "Guardias de Arequipa"

- Infantry Battalion "Iquique"

- Infantry Battalion "Guardia Civil"

- Infantry Battalion "Provisional de Lima"

- Infantry Battalion "Dos de Mayo"

- Infantry Column "Columna de Honor"

- Infantry Column "Columna Gendarmes Nacionales de Pisagua"

- Infantry Column "Columna La Noria"

- Infantry Column "Columna Naval"

- Infantry Column "Columna Naval de Pisagua"

- Infantry Column "Columna Tarapacá"

- Infantry Column "Columna Voluntarios Cerro de Pasco"

- Cavalry Squadron "Castilla"

- Cavalry Squadron "Lanceros de Tacna"

With the addition of these forces, the Peruvians were soon able to create a field army that was named "Ejercito del Sur" (Army of the South), because it had been formed in order to defend the southern provinces of the country from the Chilean aggression[21]. This field army, before being despatched to the front, was structured on six divisions: the first four were made of regular units, while the 5th and the 6th comprised National Guard corps. It is important to note that the National Guard battalions had a much more solid structure than the National Guard columns: in general, the latter were mainly formed as provisional units and usually had a small number of men, recruited as volunteers in the countryside of the Peruvian provinces. During the war, the Peruvians formed dozens of small infantry units known as "columns", but these played a very little role in the military operations, generally being broken up and used as reinforcements for existing units or as cadres to form new battalions. The "Columna de Honor", for example, was soon absorbed into the "Iquique" Battalion. As clear from the denomination of some of them, various National Guard units were made up of ex-policemen coming from the most important cities of Peru: "Guardias de Arequipa" with Arequipa policemen, "Guardia Civil" with Iquique policemen, "Columna Gendarmes Nacionales de Pisagua" with Pisagua policemen and "Columna Tarapacá" with Tarapacá policemen. To differentiate the National Guard Battalion "Ayacucho" from the regular one having the same name, the latter was re-named "1st Ayacucho" and the former "2nd Ayacucho". In addition to the "Ejercito del Sur", the Peruvians formed other two armies: the "Ejercito de Linea" (Army of the Line) and the "Ejercito de Reserva" (Army of the Reserve). The first included the few regular units that had remained in Peru to garrison the country, while the second was formed by calling to arms all the reservists in order to create a reserve force for emergencies. As a result of the defeat in the first war campaign, the "Ejercito del Sur" practically ceased to exist. Similarly, to what happened in Bolivia, the Peruvian military forces had to be completely reorganized in view of the second war campaign against Chile. Many of the original units had been routed or completely destroyed; in addition, the army needed a larger number of infantry battalions in order to face the expanded Chilean National Guard. The reorganization process was carried on under the guidance of the new Peruvian President Piérola, who decided that the Peruvian land forces had to be divided into two great administrative bodies: the "Ejercito Activo" (Active Army) and the "Ejercito de Reserva" (Reserve Army). The former was sub-divided into four field armies, each named after the area of the country where it was deployed: "Ejercito del Norte" (Army of the North), "Ejercito del Centro" (Army of the Centre), "Primero Ejercito del Sur" (First Army of the South) and "Secundo Ejercito del Sur" (Second Army of the South). The two

---

21 Estado Mayor General del Ejercito, *Historia del Ejercito de Chile*, Santiago, Chile, 1980-1983

southern armies were those effectively involved in the military operations against Chile, with the second one acting as a sort of strategic reserve for the first[22]. The Army of the Centre was mainly stationed around Lima for protection of the capital, while the Army of the North defended the Andean provinces of the north. The "Ejercito de Reserva", at least for the moment, existed only on paper. According to the new structure reported above, the "Ejercito Activo" included the following units:

- 1st Line Infantry Battalion "Zepita" (ex 2nd of the Line)

- 3rd Line Infantry Battalion "Ayacucho" (ex 3rd of the Line)

- 5th Line Infantry Battalion "Cazadores del Rímac"

- 7th Line Infantry Battalion "Victoria"

- 9th Line Infantry Battalion "Pisagua"

- 11th Line Infantry Battalion "Lima" (ex 8th of the Line)

- 13th Line Infantry Battalion "Huáscar"

- 15th Line Infantry Battalion "Cazadores del Misti"

- 17th Line Infantry Battalion "Guardias de Arequipa" (ex-National Guard)

- 19th Line Infantry Battalion "Granaderos del Cuzco"

- 21st Line Infantry Battalion "Provisional de Lima" (ex-National Guard)

- 23rd Line Infantry Battalion "Tarapacá" (ex-National Guard "Cazadores de Tarapacá")

- 25th Line Infantry Battalion "Guardias de Arequipa"

- 27th Line Infantry Battalion "Arica"

- 29th Line Infantry Battalion "Artesanos de Tacna"

- 31st Line Infantry Battalion "Granaderos de Tacna"

- 33rd Line Infantry Battalion "Iquique" (ex-National Guard)

- National Guard Infantry Battalion "Canchis"

- National Guard Infantry Battalion "Canas"

- National Guard Infantry Battalion "Cazadores de Piérola"

- National Guard Infantry Battalion "Granaderos del Cuzco"

- National Guard Infantry Battalion "Nacionales de Tacna"

- National Guard Infantry Battalion "Vengadores de Grau"

- National Guard Infantry Column "Columna Agricultores de Para"

22 Greve-Moller P., Fernàndez-Cerda C., *Uniforms of the Pacific War 1879-1884*, Nottingham, 2010

- National Guard Infantry Column "Columna Artesanos de Tacna"

- National Guard Infantry Column "Columna Guardia Civil de Moquegua"

- National Guard Infantry Column "Columna Grau"

- National Guard Infantry Column "Columna Mollendo"

- National Guard Infantry Column "Columna Policía de Tacna"

- 1st Line Cavalry Squadron "Húsares de Junín" (ex 1st Regiment of the Line)

- 3rd Line Cavalry Squadron "Guías del Perú" (ex 3rd Regiment of the Line)

- 5th Line Cavalry Squadron "Flanqueadores de Tacna"

- National Guard Cavalry Squadron "Gendarmes a Caballo de Moquegua"

- National Guard Cavalry Squadron "Lanceros de Tacna"

- National Guard Cavalry Squadron "Tiradores de Lluta"

- National Guard Cavalry Column "Columna Gendarmes de Tacna"

- 1st Artillery Brigade

- 2nd Artillery Brigade

It is interesting to note that the seventeen line infantry battalions were all numbered with odd numbers: this was made for a precise reason, because the plans of the Peruvian government contemplated the formation of an equal number of battalions from the Reserve Army, which were to be numbered with even numbers. However, at least for the moment, this plan was not put in practice and the battalions of the Active Army were the only to fight in the second war campaign. Only a very little number of units from the army of the first campaign had survived: thee infantry battalions of the line, four infantry battalions of the National Guard, Two cavalry regiments of the line and one cavalry squadron of the National Guard. The four National Guard battalions were transformed into regular ones, while the two cavalry regiments were reduced to squadrons. The artillery was also affected by this new organization: the original regiments were transformed into Artillery Brigades, which both provided the field guns for the army on campaign. It is interesting to note

The Peruvian Admiral Miguel Grau Seminario, commander of the Huáscar.

that, also this time, some new units were formed with ex-policemen: "Guardias de Arequipa" (the new one), "Columna Guardia Civil de Moquegua", "Columna Policía de Tacna", "Gendarmes a Caballo de Moquegua" and "Columna Gendarmes de Tacna". All the military forces listed above were divided among the four armies that made up the "Ejercito Activo": the "Ejercito del Norte" had five infantry divisions; the "Ejercito del Centro" had five infantry divisions and one cavalry brigade; the "Primero Ejercito del Sur" had eight infantry divisions and one cavalry division (plus the 1st Artillery Brigade); the "Secundo Ejercito del Sur" had just two infantry divisions (plus the 2nd Artillery Brigade). The Reserve Army, existing only on paper, was made up entirely of National Guard units and was to be divided between "Reserva Movilizable" (Mobilizable Reserve) and "Reserva Sedentaria" (Sedentary Reserve). Despite all the efforts made to enlarge and reorganize the army, the Peruvian military forces were again defeated and mostly destroyed by the end of the second war campaign.

THE DEFENCE OF LIMA

Following the decisive Chilean victory of Tacna, the strategic and military situation of Peru changed drastically: Bolivia was completely out of the scene and the southern provinces of Peru were in the hands of the enemy. The next objective of the Chileans was the final annihilation of the Peruvians and of their remaining military potential, so they soon planned an ambitious amphibious operation which main goal was the occupation of Lima and of central Peru[23]. President Piérola, with an army almost completely destroyed and no adequate defences around Lima, had to create new military forces from zero and in a very short time. Despite the emergency and the critical material conditions, he was able to organize an impressive military apparatus for the defence of Lima. Every human resource available was used and the population showed strong patriotic feelings: these factors, in addition to Piérola's personal energy and capabilities, enabled the Peruvians to deploy a superior number of new military units. The "Ejercito de Reserva" was finally mobilized during July-August 1880, while the "Ejercito del Norte", "Ejercito del Centro" and "Secundo Ejercito del Sur" all melted together in order to form a new and unified "Ejercito de Linea" (Army of the Line). The "Primero Ejercito del Sur", which had bore the brunt of the fighting during the previous campaign and thus had been completely destroyed, was formally disbanded. These were the orders of battle of the two new Peruvian armies:

ARMY OF THE LINE

- 1st Line Infantry Battalion "Guardia Peruana"

- 3rd Line Infantry Battalion "Cajamarca"

- 5th Line Infantry Battalion "9 de Diciembre"

- 7th Line Infantry Battalion "Tarma"

- 9th Line Infantry Battalion "Callao"

- 11th Line Infantry Battalion "Libres de Trujillo"

- 13th Line Infantry Battalion "Junín"

- 15th Line Infantry Battalion "Ica"

- 17th Line Infantry Battalion "Huánuco"

23 Lòpez-Urrutia, Carlos, *La Guerra del Pacifico 1879-1884*, Madrid, 2003

- 19th Line Infantry Battalion "Paucarpata"

- 21st Line Infantry Battalion "Libres de Cajamarca"

- 23rd Line Infantry Battalion "Jauja"

- 25th Line Infantry Battalion "Ancash"

- 27th Line Infantry Battalion "1st of Concepción"

- 29th Line Infantry Battalion "Zepita"

- 61st Line Infantry Battalion "Lima"

- 63rd Line Infantry Battalion "Canta"

- 65th Line Infantry Battalion "28 de Julio"

- 67th Line Infantry Battalion "Piura"

- 69th Line Infantry Battalion "23 de Diciembre"

- 71st Line Infantry Battalion "Libertad"

- 73rd Line Infantry Battalion "Pichincha"

- 75th Line Infantry Battalion "Piérola"

- 77th Line Infantry Battalion "La Mar"

- 79th Line Infantry Battalion "Arica"

- 81st Line Infantry Battalion "Manco Capac"

- 83rd Line Infantry Battalion "Ayacucho"

- 85th Line Infantry Battalion "Cazadores de Cajamarca"

- 87th Line Infantry Battalion "Unión"

- 89th Line Infantry Battalion "Cazadores de Junín"

- Line Cavalry Squadron "Escolta"

- Line Cavalry Regiment "Lanceros de Torata"

- National Guard Cavalry Regiment "Cazadores del Rímac"

- National Guard Cavalry Regiment "Morochucos de la Muerte"

- National Guard Cavalry Squadron "Escuadrón de Honor"

- Mountain Artillery Regiment

- Mounted Artillery Regiment

Nicolás de Piérola Villena, dictator of Peru from December 1879.

51

ARMY OF THE RESERVE

- 2nd Infantry Battalion of the Reserve

- 4th Infantry Battalion of the Reserve

- 6th Infantry Battalion of the Reserve

- 8th Infantry Battalion of the Reserve

- 10th Infantry Battalion of the Reserve

- 12th Infantry Battalion of the Reserve

- 14th Infantry Battalion of the Reserve

- 16th Infantry Battalion of the Reserve

- 18th Infantry Battalion of the Reserve

- 20th Infantry Battalion of the Reserve

- 22nd Infantry Battalion of the Reserve

- 24th Infantry Battalion of the Reserve

- 26th Infantry Battalion of the Reserve

- 28th Infantry Battalion of the Reserve

- 30th Infantry Battalion of the Reserve

- 32nd Infantry Battalion of the Reserve

- 34th Infantry Battalion of the Reserve

- 36th Infantry Battalion of the Reserve

- 38th Infantry Battalion of the Reserve

- 40th Infantry Battalion of the Reserve

- 42nd Infantry Battalion of the Reserve

- 44th Infantry Battalion of the Reserve

- 46th Infantry Battalion of the Reserve

- 48th Infantry Battalion of the Reserve

- 50th Infantry Battalion of the Reserve

- 52nd Infantry Battalion of the Reserve

- 54th Infantry Battalion of the Reserve

- 56th Infantry Battalion of the Reserve

- 58th Infantry Battalion of the Reserve

- 60th Infantry Battalion of the Reserve

- Cavalry Brigade of the Reserve

- Artillery Brigade of the Reserve

The Army of the Line comprised thirty battalions of infantry, eight squadrons of cavalry (regiments had two squadrons each) and two regiments of artillery; the Army of the Reserve had thirty battalions of infantry, one brigade of cavalry (structured on three squadrons) and one brigade of artillery. The internal organization of the two Peruvian armies was well defined: each of them had ten infantry divisions, with three battalions in each division. In addition, the ten infantry divisions of the Army of the Line were grouped into four Army Corps (of which the 1st and 4th had three divisions each and the 2nd and 3rd had two divisions each). Those of the Army of the Reserve were grouped into two Army Corps, with five divisions each. The line artillery had been re-structured on two regiments, but this time these were differentiated between mountain

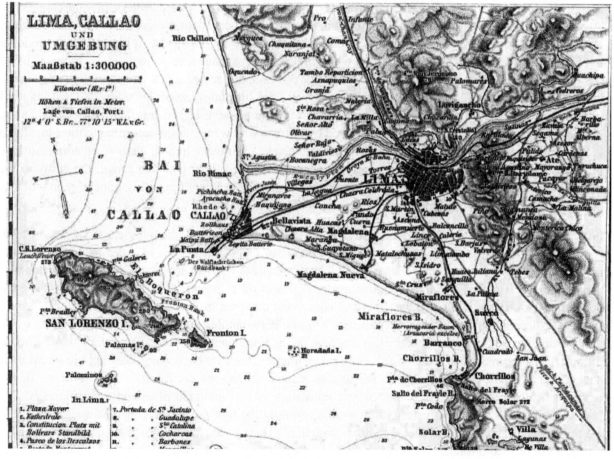

Map of Lima, showing the port of Callao and the island of San Lorenzo.

53

and mounted artillery and not more between field and fortress artillery. In fact, most of the heavy pieces mounted in the static defences of Lima and Callao were employed as normal field pieces by the Artillery Brigade of the Reserve, as well as many naval guns removed from the Peruvian warships. The Mountain Artillery Regiment transported its guns with mules, while the Mounted Artillery Regiment transported its pieces with horses (more or less as a horse artillery regiment). As clear from the numbering of the sixty infantry battalions, odd numbers were given to line units and even numbers were given to reserve units[24]. It is not clear why the numbering of the line battalions jumped from 29 to 61. The Army of the Reserve was almost entirely composed by Lima's active and sedentary reserves, which were completely mobilized by Piérola to face the military emergency. All the male inhabitants of Lima aged 16 to 60 were obliged to train between 10 a.m. and 2 p.m. during normal days; to ensure that all able-bodied reservists attended this compulsory training, the government ordered to suspend any kind of commercial occupation during those hours reserved to exercising. Only certain occupations were exempted from the compulsory training: physicians, pharmacists, clergy, health and charity workers, employees of the ministry of war or government. To avoid any kind of desertion, the government required a passport from anyone wishing to leave the province of Lima, except those involved in the transportation of foodstuffs. The ten divisions that made up the Army of the Reserve were organized on the basis of the reservists' civilian employment: 1st Division, bachelors and men involved in the legal system or legal professions; 2nd Division, property owners and men involved in commerce or finance; 3rd Division, professors and students; 4th Division, architects and men involved in the construction trade; 5th Division, men working in leather or millinery trades; 6th Division, metal workers and millers; 7th Division, printers and public or private employees; 8th Division, bakers and domestic servants; 9th Division, painters, paperhangers, upholsterers, barbers and salesmen; 10th Division, transporters, plumbers, municipal and railroad employees. Men providing livery services were assigned to the cavalry, while firemen and carriage men were assigned to the artillery. All Peruvian males, regardless of their social class or position, had to serve in the military units defending Lima: if an individual refused to train or tried to escape from his duties, he could be arrested and inducted immediately into the army. The soldiers of the Army of the Reserve lacked training, proper equipment, weapons and uniforms: in addition, they were led by officers who were chosen according to their loyalty to Piérola and not for their military capacities. Most of the veteran officers, in fact, were given administrative functions by the dictator who always feared military revolts. Considering all the above, the Army of the Reserve was an army in name only: it had large numbers, but its soldiers were not comparable in terms of quality to Baquedano's veterans who were investing the Peruvian capital.

It is interesting to note how the "Lanceros de Torata" had been re-formed; the other cavalry units, instead, were all new ones. The "Escolta" had been created as an independent unit, in order to perform as the mounted personal escort of President Piérola. The "Cazadores del Rímac" had a very peculiar history: they had been formed as a National Guard cavalry regiment on 26 March 1880, being equipped since the beginning with horses, uniforms, weapons and equipment captured from the Chileans. In fact, on 23 July 1879, a Chilean transport ship had been captured by the Peruvian fleet near the port of Antofagasta while transporting the 1st Squadron from the Cavalry Regiment "Carabineros de Yungay": with the large amount of materials captured from this ship (including 215 horses), the Peruvians were later able to equip their new National Guard cavalry regiment, which was named "Cazadores del Rímac" from the name of the captured Chilean ship. This unit included two squadrons: one of mounted rifles and one of lancers. The "Morochucos de la Muerte". Instead, they were a semi-regular unit raised from the "Morochucos", who are the Peruvian equivalent of the Argentine "gauchos". These men, famous for their boldness and hard riding, were of mixed Indian and Spanish descent; they lived with their cattle on the high plateaus of the

24 Greve-Moller P., Fernàndez-Cerda C., *Uniforms of the Pacific War 1879-1884*, Nottingham, 2010

Andes in central Peru and were perfectly skilled as light cavalry explorers and skirmishers. According to a popular legend, the "Morochucos" were the descendants of the dissident "conquistador" Diego de Almagro and of his supporters, who during 1537-1542 had fought in a brutal civil war against the Spanish colonial authorities of the newly-conquered Peruvian territory. According to popular belief, after being defeated in a decisive way, the son of Almagro and his remaining supporters fled to the Peruvian "Altiplano", where they mixed with the local Indios and created a new population known as "Pampacangallo". The Spanish exiles brought with them their excellent Andalusian horses, teaching the local Indios how to ride them. With the progression of time, the descendants of the "Pampacangallo" transformed into a race of horse breeders and the original Andalusian horses gradually adapted themselves to the environmental conditions of the Andes, becoming little but very resistant mountain horses. During the War of the Pacific, the "Morochucos" played a very important role: in fact, they were probably the best light cavalry that the Peruvian government could employ. The Regiment "Morochucos de la Muerte" was formed after the end of the second war campaign; after being created, the unit spent a month of training in Ayacucho before going to Lima in November 1880, under command of the famous and valorous Colonel Miota[25]. The "Morochucos" had no uniforms and were armed with their traditional weapons: the name of the unit, as well as the symbol on the pennant of their lances, was chosen by the same Colonel Miota and can be translated as "Morochucos of the Death". After the Chilean occupation of Lima, these cowboys continued to fight for their homeland, being a decisive component of the resistance forces that continued the fight against the invaders in the so-called "Sierra Campaign". In addition to the units listed in the previous orders of battle, the Peruvians deployed also a certain number of independent corps, many of which had special functions:

- National Guard Infantry Battalion "Columna Celadores"

- National Guard Infantry Battalion "Camaleros"

- National Guard Infantry Battalion "Depósito y Guarnición"

- National Guard Infantry Battalion "Guardia Chalaca"

- National Guard Infantry Battalion "Guarnición de Marina"

- National Guard Infantry Battalion "Voluntarios de Canta"

- National Guard Infantry Column "Columna de Honor"

- National Guard Infantry Column "Columna Guías"

- National Guard Infantry Column "Columna Pachacamac"

- "Columna Policía de Seguridad de Lima" (three battalions, with five companies in total)

- "Morochucos" (engineers/sappers)

The "Columna Celadores" was a unit composed by ex-policemen, something very common in the armies that fought in the War of the Pacific. "Celadores" was one of the many different terms used to indicate policemen, who could be known as "Guardias", "Gendarmes", "Policía" or "Guardia Civil". The "celadores", in particular, were a sort of municipal guard whose main function was to maintain order in urban centres. The "Camaleros", instead, were public officers who were responsable for supervising the butchering process of cattle. In practice, the "camaleros" were those public workers who transformed the herds of cattle into meat for the large population of the Peruvian capital. We know very little about the unit

---

25 Greve-Moller P., Fernàndez-Cerda C., *Uniformes de la Guerra del Pacifico 1879-1884*, Santiago, Chile, 2008

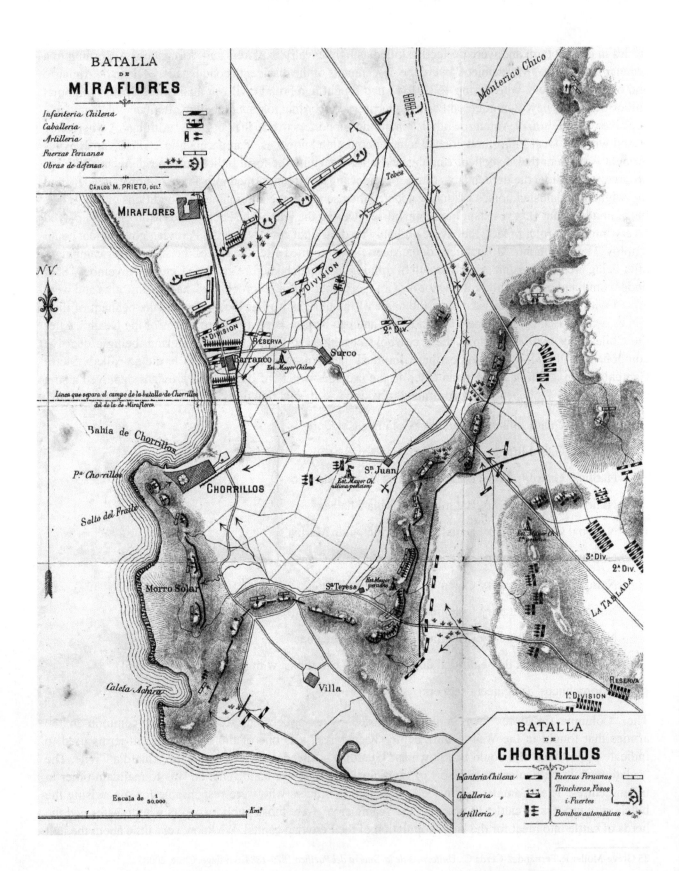

BATALLA
DE
MIRAFLORES

Infanteria Chilena
Caballeria „
Artilleria „
Fuerzas Peruanas
Obras de defensa

CARLOS M. PRIETO, DELT.

MIRAFLORES

N.V.

1ª DIVISION

2ª DIV.

3ª DIVISION

RESERVA

Surco

Barranco

Est. Mayor Chileno

Linea que separa el campo de la batalla de Chorrillos del de la de Miraflores.

Bahía de Chorrillos

Pª Chorrillos

CHORRILLOS

Salto del Fraile

Morro Solar

Caleta Achira

Villa

Sn Juan

Est. Mayor Ch. ultima pantalon

Sª Teresa

Est. Mayor peruano

Est. Mayor Ch. 1ª pantalon

Montevideo Chico

Tebes

3ª Div.

2ª Div.

LA TABLADA

RESERVA

1ª DIVISION

BATALLA
DE
CHORRILLOS

Infanteria Chilena
Caballeria „
Artilleria „

Fuerzas Peruanas
Trincheras, Fosos i Fuertes
Bombas automáticas

Escala de 1/50,000

Km.ᵗ

56

known as "Depósito y Guarnición": judging from the name, it is highly probable that it was a static unit composed by veterans and invalids, who acted as deposit and garrison forces. The "Voluntarios de Canta" were a battalion of volunteers coming from one of the provinces that made up the department of Lima, located just north of the Peruvian capital. The "Columna de Honor", was a small provisional unit composed by officers coming from the reserve or by officers whose original unit was no longer in existence. The "Columna Guías" was probably a small temporary unit of semi-regular scouts and explorers, while the "Columna Pachacamac" was a little corps of volunteers coming from the city of Pachacamac, located 40 km south-east of Lima and famous for its ancient Inca ruins. The "Morochucos" were nothing else than the old "Morochucos de la Muerte" who, at a certain point of the campaign, had their firearms taken away and started to be employed as engineers/sappers for maintenance of the defensive lines at Chorrillos and Miraflores.

The "Guardia Chalaca" and "Guarnición de Marina", instead, had a common and very interesting history. After defeat in the second war campaign, it soon became clear to Piérola and his officers that the Chileans were going to organize a large expedition with the intention of conquering Lima. For this reason, the Peruvian high command soon started to form new units for the defence of the capital and of its strategic port of Callao. The latter was the largest port of Peru and one of the most important in South America: all the Peruvian commercial routes with Europe passed through this strategic centre, which control was fundamental for the prosecution of the hostilities. Since 10 April 1880, after defeating the Peruvian naval forces in various engagements, the Chilean Navy blockaded the port of Callao, preventing the remaining Peruvian warships from going in the Pacific Ocean. The main objective of the blockade was that of gradually stifling Peruvian trade and contacts with the rest of the world, in order to destroy the Peruvian economy. During the months that preceded the Chilean offensive against Lima, the inhabitants of Callao (commonly known as "chalacos") launched many courageous but vane night attacks against the Chilean warships blockading the port: these small raids, made with little boats, had no chance of success against the Chilean fleet but were very important to keep the moral high ground[26]. When Piérola mobilized the population of Lima for the defence of the city against the approaching Chileans, the port of Callao obviously contributed, by creating two units: the "Guardia Chalaca" and the "Guarnición de Marina". The two battalions were composed by men living or working in the port, especially by members of the "Cuartel" and "Arsenal" (respectively the Base and Arsenal of the Peruvian Navy). In normal life the soldiers of these two units were shipwrights, custom agents, firemen, fishermen, traders and longshoremen who now all wanted to defend their port and homeland. Many of them had already fought as seamen or during the night raids launched against the Chilean naval blockade. By the time of the War of the Pacific, the Peruvians no longer had a unit of naval infantry: in fact, in the years that preceded the conflict, the Battalion "Lima" (the 8th of the Line Infantry) had performed many of the duties that would have been specific of a proper naval infantry unit. With the formation of the "Guardia Chalaca" and "Guarnición de Marina", the Peruvians finally had two new and strong units for defence of the Callao and of their remaining warships. The "Guardia Chalaca" was structured as a battalion with three companies, while the "Guarnición de Marina" had a total of 524 men divided into six companies. Because of its strong establishment, the latter unit was sometimes referred to as "brigade"; its officers all came from the regular Army or from the Navy, while its rankers included also a certain number of survivors from the regular infantry battalions destroyed during the previous war campaign. Under many points of view, both the battalions formed with "chalacos" were elite units: however, unluckily for them, they were employed as normal infantry in the terrible battle of Miraflores. Both units were totally destroyed in the clash: no one of their members survived, including the two valorous commanders.

---

26 Estado Mayor General del Ejercito, *Historia del Ejercito de Chile*, Santiago, Chile, 1980-1983

The "Columna Policía de Seguridad de Lima" was a police unit specifically created to maintain public order in the city of Lima during the third war campaign against the Chileans. The history of the Peruvian police during the years of the War of the Pacific was very complicated: the police corps of the largest towns, in fact, were largely employed to form new National Guard units. In 1873 the Peruvian government had completely reformed its police corps; according to the "Reforma Policial" of that year, the Peruvian police forces were to be divided into two main branches of service: the "Gendarmeria" and the "Guardia Civil". The first had a more military nature, because it had the usual functions of a normal police corps but could perform auxiliary military duties in case of war with a foreign country. The "Guardia Civil", instead, was more a civil corps of police acting as a sort of urban guard (also in the smallest towns and villages of the country). The "Gendarmeria" was formed as early as 1853 by President Benavente, comprising eight foot companies and one mounted regiment with four squadrons (specifically created for service in Lima). The "Guardia Civil" came into being only with the important reform of 1873, issued by President Pardo. In general terms, the "Gendarmeria" had to protect public buildings, functionaries of the state and guard the prisoners in public jails. The "Guardia Civil" had to protect private citizens and their properties. Both kinds of policemen were deployed in all the departments of Peru; shortly after the 1873 reform, the Peruvian police forces numbered a total of 1,552 men (912 of the "Guardia Civil" and 640 of the "Gendarmeria"). When war broke out, all the military units that garrisoned Lima were sent to the front in order to fight against Chile. As a result, the policemen remained as the only force that could maintain order in the large and over-populated Peruvian capital. When the Chilean invading army approached Lima, in order to contain any eventual riot and maintain internal stability, Piérola ordered a general reorganization of the city's police forces, which were strongly militarized. They were united into a new force known as "Columna Policía de Seguridad de Lima", structured on three battalions: the first and second battalion had two companies each (also known as "columns" and being identified with capital letters), while the third battalion had just one company. However, to reinforce the Peruvian defensive line at Chorrillos, Lima's policemen were sent to the front, leaving the city with no public force for the internal security.

During the night between the Battle of Miraflores and the Chilean entrance into the city (16-17 January 1881), a large group of stragglers and deserters from the defeated Peruviana Army entered Lima: these men killed, looted and burned everything for some hours without any serious opposition from the urban authorities. Benefiting from this confused situation, many of the city's criminals joined the parties of rogue soldiers and proved to be particularly violent. The city's mayor, Rufino Torrico, soon understood that exceptional measures had to be taken: some sort of police force had to be formed as soon as possible, in order to save Lima from complete destruction. Since the 1860s, Lima had some companies of volunteer firemen: interestingly, these were mostly composed of foreigners. This was a tradition dating back to the year 1866, when the first volunteer company of firemen was formed with Italian immigrants living in the port of Callao. At that time Peru was at war with Spain as part of the Chincha Islands War; the Spanish fleet had already bombarded the Chilean port of Valparaiso and the Peruvians feared a similar attack against their vital port of Callao. As a result, the first company of volunteer firemen was formed, being composed by Italians living in the port (mostly fishermen). The Italian firemen performed particularly well when the Spanish attack finally materialised, with the result that other three volunteer companies of Italian firemen were formed during the years 1868-1873. The other foreign communities living in Lima, most notably the French and English ones, followed the example of the Italians and formed their own companies of firemen. All the inhabitants of Lima, as well as Rufino Torrico, had complete trust in the foreign firemen: for this reason, the mayor ordered the formation of a new police corps known as "Guardia Urbana" (Urban Guard), which was to be composed by three companies of firemen. Each of the three companies was of a different nationality, as clear from their names: "Roma", "France" and "Británica Victoria". All the foreign firemen of the three companies were soon armed and sent to fight against the rebelling slaves and disbanded soldiers; in doing this the European immigrants showed all their courage, being able to defeat the bands of criminals while at the same time extinguishing the large fires that were destroying the city. When the Chileans entered the city on the following day, public order had been mostly restored. Other two companies of Italian firemen, the "Italia" and "Garibaldi", had already taken part to the battles of Chorrillos and Miraflores: not as soldiers but as stretcher bearers to help the many wounded Peruvians. The formation of the "Guardia Urbana" by Torrico, however, was not something completely new: since the departure of Lima's garrison to the front of war in 1879, the foreign communities of Lima had started to organize themselves for the defence of their members and of their private properties[27]. For this reason, as an auxiliary force to the "Gendarmeria" and "Guardia Civil" of the city, the foreigners of Lima had already formed a "Guardia Urbana": each foreign community had organized a company with its own officers and uniforms, with the objective of helping

Francisco García-Calderón, provisional President of Peru during March-November 1881.

the police in the defence of private properties. Shortly before the Chilean attack against Lima, however, Piérola had ordered the disbandment of the "Guardia Urbana" as a measure to find new men available for military service. So the provisional Urban Guard formed in January 1881 was just the updated version of a corps that had already existed for several months.

THE ARMY OF THE CENTRE

After the disastrous defeats of Chorrillos and Miraflores, the Peruvian military forces practically ceased to exist: both the Army of the Line and the Army of the Reserve had been completely annihilated by the Chileans, with the result that the new resistance forces that were forming to oppose the invaders had to be built up from zero. Despite the occupation of Lima, a certain number of veteran officers managed to escape from the conquered city and went to the central Andes in order to organize the local resistance forces. Peru is a country with a very large territory, mostly covered by extremely high mountains: the perfect kind of terrain to confront a foreign invader with guerrilla methods. The Chileans had control of southern Peru and of Lima's surroundings: the central and northern parts of the country were still in the hands of Peruvian forces. The latter, however, consisted just of some policemen since almost every military unit had already been employed against the Chileans. Among those few officers who escaped to the central Andes was the future leader of the Peruvian resistance, Colonel Andrés Avelino Cáceres. He was without a doubt the best Peruvian commander in the War of the Pacific, having great personal capabilities and tactical sense. At the beginning of the conflict Cáceres was commander of the 2nd Line Infantry Battalion "Zepita", which under

27 Greve-Moller P., Fernàndez-Cerda C., *Uniforms of the Pacific War 1879-1884*, Nottingham, 2010

his guidance became one of the best Peruvian units[28]. During the first land campaign he was a divisional commander in the Army of the South, taking part to all the most important battles and always demonstrating great valour. At the head of the "Zepita" Battalion he took part in the second land campaign, fighting with incredible courage at the Battle of Tacna. At the Battle of Chorrillos Cáceres commanded the IV Corps of the Army of the Line, while at the Battle of Miraflores he led the 5th Division of the Army of the Reserve. In both clashes Cáceres' troops performed better than any other Peruvian military unit, but the Army of the Line was destroyed at Chorrillos and the Army of the Reserve was annihilated at Miraflores. Wounded during the second battle, Cáceres had to hide himself in order to avoid capture by the Chileans, who were searching for him. While still recovering he escaped to Jauja in the central Andes on 15 April 1881. During the following weeks Cáceres was made supreme commander of central Peru from President Piérola and received the new rank of General. The nucleus of what became his army was composed by just a few veteran officers and soldiers (many of whom were recovering in the hospital of Jauja):

- In Jauja: 33 men of the 13th Line Infantry Battalion "Junín", 65 men of the Line Cavalry Squadron "Escolta", 16 gendarmes and 19 officers all grouped into a provisional battalion known as "Constancia";

- In Tarma: 61 local policemen assembled into an infantry column;

- In Ayacucho: 100 local policemen assembled into an infantry column.

Thanks to his natural capabilities of military leader, Cáceres was soon able to assemble a good number of new recruits and form an effective (albeit small) fighting force. In this difficult process he received decisive help from the Peruvian Church, whose leaders were strongly in favour of the prosecution of hostilities against Chile. The area of Peru where Cáceres established his headquarters was mostly inhabited by the Quechua Indians, a people of hardened mountaineers representing Peru's most important native population. Cáceres was extremely popular among the Quechua Indians, because of the great courage he showed in battle and of his deep respect towards the traditions of the natives living on the mountains. He spoke Quechua language perfectly and had a great knowledge of the mountaineers' way of life. In a few months, with the help of the local clergy and landowners, Cáceres was able to create a new military force known as "Ejército del Centro" (Army of the Centre) and numbering around 3,000 men. The majority of these were Indians, commonly known as "breñeros" (mountaineers): at the orders of Cáceres (called by them "Taita", which meant "Father") the Quechua natives demonstrated to be splendid fighters, having unwavering loyalty and incredible resilience. The army expanded also thanks to the incorporation of some surviving elements from the regular forces, which formed a nucleus of well-trained veterans around which Cáceres could organize his forces on a much more solid base. The structure of the "Ejército del Centro" was as follows:

- 1st Infantry Battalion "Tarapacá" (with soldiers from the 61st Line Battalion "Lima")

- 2nd Infantry Battalion "Zepita" (with soldiers from the 23rd Line Battalion "Jauja")

- 3rd Infantry Battalion "Junín" (with soldiers from the 13th Line Battalion "Junín")

- 4th Infantry Battalion "Pucará" (initially named "Ica")

- 5th Infantry Battalion "Canta" (initially named "Huancayo")

- 6th Infantry Battalion "Marcavalle"

---

28 Ejército del Peru, *Evolucion Historica de los Uniformes del Ejercito del Peru (1821-1980)*, Lima, Peru, 2005

- 7th Infantry Battalion "Concepción" (initially named "Tarma")

- 8th Infantry Battalion "Apata"

- 9th Infantry Battalion "Jauja" (initially named "Alianza")

- 10th Infantry Battalion "Huacho" (later named "San Geronimo")

- 11th Infantry Battalion "Tarma"

- 12th Infantry Battalion "América"

- Infantry Battalion "Ayacucho" (also known as "Libres de Ayacucho")

- Infantry Battalion "Huancavélica"

- Cavalry Squadron "Cazadores del Peru"

- Cavalry Squadron "Tarma"

- Cavalry Squadron "2 de Mayo"

- Artillery Brigade

Originally there had been two battalions named "Canta", formed together and differentiated by consecutive numbers; later they were merged together to form the single 5th Infantry Battalion "Canta". The "Ayacucho" and "Huancavélica" were not sequentially numbered, since they were not considered as part of the "line" units: it is possible that these two battalions were only semi-regular ones. For a certain period of time there was also another one of such units, named "Izcuchaca". The organization of the cavalry changed several times, since it initially comprised a single squadron named "Escolta" serving as Cáceres' mounted escort. Despite being formally organized as a regular military force, the Army of the Centre was mostly a "guerrilla" fighting force with irregular nature: Cáceres grouped his Indians into small units, formed according to their communities of origin and to the kind of weapons that they carried. Each "guerrilla" (group of irregular fighters) was under command of a regular officer or civilian representative. The Quechua Indians had joined Cáceres mainly to defend their villages and mountain valleys from Chilean occupation: for this reason, they were quite reluctant to act as a manoeuvring force outside the particular territory in which they lived. Thanks to training and the introduction of discipline, however, Peruvian officers were gradually able to improve this situation and transform the Army of the Centre into a semi-regular force. The respect and affection of both the Quechua Indians and local farmers were decisive for Cáceres' victories over the Chileans[29], who sent several expeditions from Lima with the objective of defeating the Peruvian resistance forces. Thanks to a perfect knowledge of terrain and the material support of the local population, Cáceres was able to resist for years until the final defeat of Huamachuco. The rapid attacks, surprise incursions and skirmishes launched by the "breñeros" caused serious problems to the Chileans, during the fourth land campaign of the war that was known as "Sierra" or "La Breña" Campaign because of the mountain terrain over which it was fought. Cáceres became known as the "Wizard of the Andes" because of his capability to disappear and avoid confrontation with superior enemy forces: to achieve this, he usually marched with his forces to altitudes that were not sustainable for the Chileans (who were thus forced to abandon their pursuit).

---

29 Lòpez-Urrutia, Carlos, *La Guerra del Pacifico 1879-1884*, Madrid, 2003

Admiral Lizardo Montero Flores, legitimate President of Peru from November 1881.

THE ARMY OF THE NORTH

The Army of the Centre was not the only resistance force organized to to go against the Chileans: in the northern provinces of Peru, in fact, a similar military force named "Ejército del Norte" (Army of the North) was formed under the leadership of Miguel Iglesias[30]. The latter had been one of Piérola's most important supporters during his ascendancy to power and had been among the most important Peruvian military commanders during the previous war campaigns. During the defence of Lima, Iglesias had been commander of the I Corps of the Army of the Line at Chorrillos, where he was captured by the Chileans. Iglesias, however, was soon freed in order to report the conditions of surrender offered by the Chilean high command to the Peruvians. After performing this function, Iglesias remained for a brief period in Lima when the city was occupied by the Chileans. Having showed a certain positive attitude towards the invaders, he obtained for himself to retire to private life and leaved Lima for his large estates located in the northern province of Cajamarca. Meanwhile Lizardo Montero had replaced Piérola as President of Peru and was now forming a new government with the intention of continuing the fight against the Chileans. He went to the city of Arequipa in the south, which was still in Peruvian hands, and assumed command of the local garrison. The new government was recognized by Cáceres, while the same Montero nominated Iglesias as supreme commander of northern Peru (February 1882). As a result Iglesias started to organize his "Ejército del Norte" in order to face the Chileans. As Cáceres in the central areas of Peru, he had to build his new military units practically from zero. The majority of the new recruits came from the province of Cajamarca, where Iglesias had his land properties and powerbase. The contribution of ex-regular soldiers was very scarce, since no surviving units had been able to escape in the north. The order of battle of the Army of the North was as follows:

- 1st Line Infantry Battalion "Trujillo"

- 2nd Line Infantry Battalion "Callao"

- Infantry Column "Libres de Trujillo"

- Infantry Column "Chota"

- Infantry Column "Bambamarca"

- Infantry Column "Huaigayoc"

- Infantry Column "San Miguel"

- Infantry Column "Llapa"

- Infantry Column "Honor de Cajamarca"

- Cavalry Squadron "Vengadores de Cajamarca"

- Artillery Brigade

General Cáceres, leader of the Peruvian resistance forces during the fourth war campaign.

This small force, numbering more or less 600 men, was able to win a minor battle against the Chileans at San Pablo on 13 July 1882 (not far from the estates of Iglesias). Shortly after this success, however, Iglesias' small army was defeated by the Chileans and the province

30 Estado Mayor General del Ejercito, *Historia del Ejercito de Chile*, Santiago, Chile, 1980-1983

of Cajamarca was occupied and sacked by the foreign invaders. After this defeat Iglesias became strongly convinced that peace with Chile was the only realistic way to save Peru from complete destruction. For this reason, in August he issued a manifesto calling for peace, known as "Grito de Montán": this, however, was rejected by Cáceres and Montero who continued to fight against the Chileans (they did not want to accept any territorial concession to the enemy). At this point Iglesias decided to continue on his way and started official peace talks with the Chileans, after proclaiming himself Supreme Commander of Peru. To have some legitimacy at the eyes of the Peruvian people, he called a convention of political representatives from the seven departments of northern Peru in December 1882; on 1 January 1883 the northern representatives proclaimed Iglesias "Regenerating President of Peru" and charged him to conclude a definitive peace treaty with the Chileans. The latter soon understood that Iglesias was the only possible negotiator who could help them to achieve a positive end of the conflict: for this reason they started to officially support him during February 1883. Meanwhile Cáceres, who by now considered Iglesias as a traitor, was planning to send part of his forces against him in the north. Thanks to the Chilean help Iglesias was able to reform his Northern Army[31], this time on a smaller but more solid basis:

- 1st Line Infantry Battalion "Regenerador"

- 2nd Line Infantry Battalion "Cajamarca"

- Artillery Brigade

On 10 July 1883 Cáceres' Army of the Centre was decisively defeated at Huamachuco; this event led to the signing of the Treaty of Ancón between Chile and Peru (on 20 October 1883), which was signed by Iglesias as Provisional President of Peru and brought the War of the Pacific to an end. On 24 October Montero surrendered in Arequipa with the military forces under his command. Iglesias' troops were the first to enter Lima after the Chileans abandoned the city, but their apparent success was not to last for long. Soon after the end of the War of the Pacific, civil war erupted in Peru between Iglesias and Cáceres. Initially the Army of the North (by now also known as "Provisional Army") was able to defeat and contrast the Army of the Centre, but on 3 December 1885 Cáceres was finally able to defeat Iglesias in Lima and became the new President of Peru. Iglesias went into exile in Spain and his Army of the North was disbanded. Cáceres remained as the only master of Peru and his Army of the Centre acted as the main core around which the new Peruvian Army was built.

General Miguel Iglesias, "regenerating" President of Peru from January 1883.

31 Greve-Moller P., Fernàndez-Cerda C., *Uniforms of the Pacific War 1879-1884*, Nottingham, 2010

THE ARMY OF AREQUIPA

The Battle of Tacna, fought on 26 May 1880, was one of the most decisive moments in the War of the Pacific: it brought the second war campaign to an end and led to the definitive withdrawal of Bolivia from the conflict. With that defeat, both the Bolivian Army and the Peruvian Army of the South were practically destroyed: the remnants of the Peruvian forces, however, were able to retreat and entrenched themselves in the important southern city of Arequipa. They remained here for the rest of the war, without taking part to any further action and simply acting as the normal military garrison of the city. Meanwhile the Chileans launched their campaign against Lima, so the military operations were definitively transferred to the heart of Peru. Arequipa remained in Peruvian hands and the Chileans did not plan any operation against the enemy city, since its garrison (albeit large) was not considered to be a menace. The Chileans had other priorities and their main objective was conquering the capital of Peru. As we have previously said, when chosen as new President of Peru, Lizardo Montero moved to Arequipa and took command of the local forces. These were known as "Army of Arequipa" and included the following units:

- 3rd Line Infantry Battalion "Ayacucho" (surviving unit from the Army of the South)

- 11th Line Infantry Battalion "Lima" (surviving unit from the Army of the South)

- Infantry Battalion "Grau" (ex "Columna Grau", surviving from the Army of the South)

- Infantry Battalion "Apurimac"

- Infantry Battalion "2 de Mayo"

- Infantry Battalion "Libres del Cuzco"

- Infantry Battalion "Tarapacá"

- Infantry Battalion "Legión Peruana"

- Infantry Battalion "Piquiza"

- Infantry Battalion "Piérola"

- Infantry Battalion "Paruro"

- Infantry Battalion "Andahuaylas"

- Cavalry Squadron "Húsares de Junín" (surviving unit from the Army of the South)

- Cavalry Squadron "Guías" (surviving unit from the Army of the South)

- Artillery Brigade

After signing of the Treaty of Ancón between Chile and Peru (20 October 1883), Lizardo Montero tried to resist in Arequipa with this army that numbered more or less 4,000 men. However, when a Chilean expedition of just 3,000 soldiers approached the city, the garrison and inhabitants revolted against the President and obliged him to cancel any plan of further resistance. Arequipa was finally occupied by the Chileans on 24 October without a fight and Montero fled to asylum in Bolivia. The last Peruvian stronghold in the War of the Pacific had fallen.

FORMATION AND COMPOSITION

During the first years of its existence, the Peruvian Army did not have a military academy for the formation of officers[32]: this lack of training, however, soon became apparent during the war fought against Gran Colombia in 1828-1829. As a result, on 30 January 1830, President Gamarra ordered the creation of the first Peruvian military academy. Unfortunately, due to the political problems that characterised the first decades of Peruvian history, this was active only sporadically. After some years of good service, it was closed for a first time in 1834. On 7 January 1850 President Castilla opened again the academy, which was now named "Instituto Militar"; this was closed between Castilla's first and second period of rule, being finally transformed into a more stable institution in 1859. At this time, however, the military academy continued to suffer from the continuous political unrest, working properly only until 1867 when it was again closed. In 1872 the military academy was re-opened as part of the new general measures introduced to modernise the Peruvian Army, which included the adoption of more modern weapons acquired from Europe and the introduction of new dress regulations in French style. President Pardo (the first civilian president in the history of Peru) ordered the opening of the new "Military College" on 1 October 1872, which was followed on 24 July 1873 by the new "Escuela de Clases". The latter was a military school created for training of NCOs; Pardo's objective was that of reconstructing the Peruvian military leadership gradually and from zero, creating a competent body of officers and NCOs who would have been capable of modernizing the armed forces from the inside. Despite the efforts of Pardo's government, the quality of the Peruvian officers who marched to the front in 1879 was still very low.

The number of officers who had graduated before the outbreak of the hostilities was very small, since the first class of the new military academy had graduated only in 1877. The same could be said of the "Escuela de Clases", with the result that the Peruvian Army suffered from a chronic lack of competent sergeants and corporals. The majority of the officers who took part to the first two campaigns of the War of the Pacific had built up their careers during the military coups and revolutions of the previous decades, thus obtaining their positions thanks to the loyalty shown to the various political leaders (and not for their state of service or military competence).

In 1878 the Peruvian Army included a total of 2,679 officers, much more than the number effectively needed: to make a simple comparison, Peru had six times as many officers as the Chilean Army. In addition, a large number of these officers did not serve with any of the units, 960 of them being actually defined as having a "licencia indefinida" (indefinite licence). These were "parasite" surplus officers who were regularly paid (although receiving a reduced salary) despite having no definite function or command. The number of Peruvian officers had become so large as a result of the military's

General Juan Buendía, commander of the Allied Army during the first war campaign.

---

32 Sater, William F., *Andean Tragedy: Fighting the War of the Pacific 1879–1884*, University of Nebraska, 2007

66

continuous involvement in politics: the political scene of Peru had been dominated by the military elites since the country's independence, with the majority of the various governments being formed and guided by generals as the result of military coups or civil wars. In practice, civilians had a quite insignificant role in the administration of the state: the military leadership was generally in total control, albeit being always divided between the faction actually holding power and the opposite one wishing to take the former's place. The officers of the ruling faction had complete salaries and active commands; those of the defeated faction were the "indefinidos", who received a reduced pay and had no effective functions. As a result, Peru was always on the verge of civil war and the officer corps was strongly divided due to political questions. Bearing all this in mind, it is easy to understand why the Peruvian officers performed so badly during the War of the Pacific. All this had also other important consequences: the cost of maintaining such a massive military bureaucracy absorbed a large portion of the Peruvian state's income, which could have been used for other purposes.

Peru had a conscription law as most of the other South American countries of the time, introduced in 1872, but this was only honoured on paper. According to the law, military service was mandatory for all able-bodied men aged 21 or older. Each man, however, had the possibility to buy a replacement in order to avoid service in the army. Once enlisted, each soldier had to serve for three years in the active army and two in the reserve. In practice, however, this system soon proved to be a total failure and the army continued to suffer from a great lack of manpower: as a result, the Peruvian government abandoned conscription and decided to entice men into enlisting voluntarily for smaller periods of service (two years for the infantry, three for cavalry and artillery). At the end of this period of volunteer service, each soldier was to receive a bonus payment that he could use for his civilian life (for any kind of investment). This new recruiting system, however, proved to be inadequate with the progression of the hostilities. As had already happened in the past, the Peruvian government started to resort to more unorthodox methods for fillings the ranks of the army: since whites were generally able to find a way for avoiding military service, the burden of fighting fell upon people of color (blacks and Indians). Thousands of Indians from the interior provinces were forcibly recruited and sent to Lima, but at the first occasion these recruits were ready to desert and go back to their homes[33].

Press-gangs were regularly sent to the small rural villages inhabited by natives, with the result of producing further hate against Lima's dictatorial government. As we have already seen, Indians will later show great patriotism and valour when defending their homes under the competent and respectful guide of Cáceres. In general terms the Peruvian common soldier had the same basic capacities of the Chilean equivalent, but was largely inferior for what regarded dress, equipment and weapons. In addition, the bad military preparation of the officers prevented the Peruvian recruits from transforming into a good fighting force. Because of their usual harsh life-style, Peruvian rankers had the potential to perform very well on the field of battle, if obviously properly trained and led. They were accustomed to walk for miles in harsh terrain and had great resilience, being able to fight also after very long marches conducted with personal equipment (in particular shoes) of scarce quality. Many of the Peruvian Indians had not a very clear idea about the function of the war against Chile: this obviously had negative consequences over their performances in battle, since morale was almost always very low. The Peruvian cavalry had more or less the same problems of the infantry, especially regarding poor equipment and weapons. The few available horses, in addition, were of very low quality. The Peruvian authorities prohibited Indians from serving in the cavalry due to ancient prejudices and thus the mounted units were mostly composed by blacks and "mestizos". The same happened also for the artillery.

---

33 Lòpez-Urrutia, Carlos, *La Guerra del Pacifico 1879-1884*, Madrid, 2003

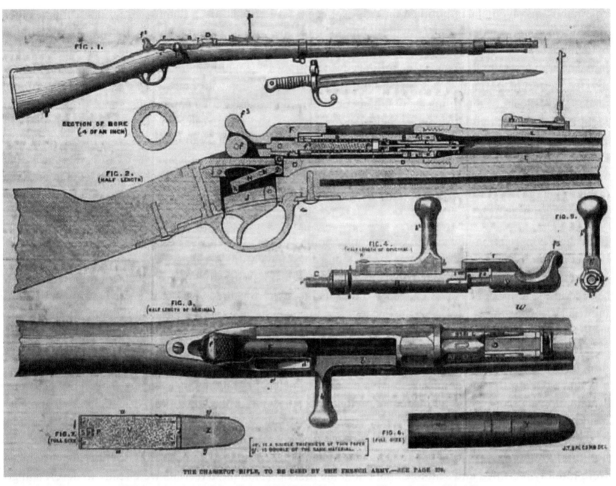

The mechanism of the French M1866 Chassepot rifle, employed by Peru.

WEAPONS

After the end of the Chincha Islands War against Spain (1864-1866), the Peruvian government decided to start modernizing the weaponry of the infantry units. At that time the Peruvian infantrymen were still mostly armed with old percussion muskets, Austrian or Prussian Minié-type weapons imported from Europe or local copies of them. The process of modernization started with the acquisition of a certain number of M1866 Snider-Enfield rifles, manufactured in the USA and probably surplus ones of the Civil War. Obviously this first purchase was not enough, since Peruvian infantry had to be totally re-equipped. In 1869 a first military mission was sent to Europe by the Peruvian government with the objective of buying new rifles for the army; the result of this first commercial tour was the acquisition of 5,000 M1866 Chassepot rifles, manufactured for the Peruvians in Belgium by the Gillion factory. These weapons, however, soon proved to be defective: as a result, in 1870 the Peruvian government had to buy more rifles from Europe, these being 2,000 Belgian Comblains II. Obviously, the Peruvian high command was not yet satisfied by these acquisitions, also because the Chassepots and Comblains had different calibres and this was going to cause great confusion regarding the supply of ammunitions. To alleviate this problem in 1873 the Peruvians sent a second military mission to Europe, with the objective of concluding a contract with one of the major factories producing weapons for export. This new delegation was led by the competent Colonel Castañon, whose first attempt was that of buying more exemplars of the excellent Comblain II rifle (which in 1871 had been adopted as

68

Photo of a M1874 Turkish Peabody-Martini rifle, employed by Peru.

standard weapon of the Belgian Army). However, this was not possible due to the fact that the Belgian factory had already accepted large commissions from other two South American countries: Brazil and Chile, in fact, had decided to re-equip their armies with M1870 Comblain II rifles. At this point Castañon had to search for a new solution and this resulted in a compromise: he contacted the Bornmüller factory in Germany and agreed with it to start the production of a new model of rifle, designed by the same Colonel and thus commonly known as "Castañon rifle" or "El Peruano"[34]. In practice this was nothing more than a Chassepot rifle modified to have the same calibre of the Comblain and thus use the same brass cartridges. According to the contract signed with Bonrmüller factory, the 5,000 M1866 Chassepot rifles bought in 1869 were to be sent in Europe to be modified with the new "Castañon" system. By the outbreak of the war, however, only 2,000 of them had been converted. When the conflict broke out in 1879, all the Peruvian rifles were in bad condition and many of them were defective. The use of so many different weapons (M1866 Snider-Enfield's, M1866 Chassepots, M1870 Comblains, Castañon rifles and modified M1866 Chassepots) led to an incredible confusion and enormous difficulties regarding the supply of ammunitions. The Peruvian high command claimed that by September 1879 it had standardized the weapons of the infantry, to the point that at least each division used the same firearms: this was absolutely false, as the logistical problems suffered in practice were soon to show. With the expansion of the National Guard following the declaration of war, also the old Austrian and Prussian Miniés muskets were brought back into use, being given to the new units of National Guard infantry. With the progression of hostilities, the Peruvian government was obliged to buy thousands of new rifles from other manufacturers, thus augmenting logistical problems to an almost unsustainable level. The new weapons were mostly M1874 Turkish Peabody-Martini rifles and M1871 Spanish Remingtons. Unable to purchase Martini–Henry rifles from the British because their entire production was going to re-equip British troops, Ottoman Turkey had purchased weapons identical to the British Mark I from the Providence Tool Company in Rhode Island (the manufacturers of the somewhat similar Peabody rifle). The Ottomans used them effectively against the Russians in the Russo-Turkish War of 1877-1878; at the end of the conflict, however, the Russians sold thousands of captured Turkish rifles to the Americans; the latter, in turn, sold them to the Peruvians. In addition to the M1871 Spanish Remingtons, 1,500 of which were sent by Honduras as payment for an old debt, the Peruvians employed also 5,000 M1868 Egyptian Remingtons that had been bought by the government of Costa Rica and were later given to Peru as payment for an old debt (as for Honduras). To all this we should add that captured Chilean weapons were generally re-used, especially Comblain rifles. Peruvian officers mostly used Lefaucheux and Colt revolvers; in addition, during his commercial

Colt M1873, used by Chilean and Peruvian officers as a privately-purchased weapon.

34 Greve-Moller P., Fernàndez-Cerda C., *Uniforms of the Pacific War 1879-1884*, Nottingham, 2010

journey in Germany, Castañon had bought 1,000 pistols from the Zöller factory (designed by him and thus known as "Peruvian model"). Cavalry used a variety of carbines, including Winchester, Remington and Henry ones (M1866 Winchesters being the most common)[35]. Old British M1796 light cavalry sabres were very popular.

At the beginning of the war the Peruvian artillery had 28 British-made Blakely mountain guns in various calibres, plus four 8cm Krupp M1867 field guns and twelve 6cm Krupp M1873 mountain guns. The Blakely muzzle-loading guns were quite old, having been bought in 1866 for the Chincha Islands War (presumably surplus of the US Civil War). The artillery included also four Gatling machine guns: others of these were purchased during the war, together with Claxton, Gardner and Nordenfeldt ones. The forty-eight Peruvian pieces (forty-four guns and four machine guns) were organized into six batteries having eight pieces each. Single artillerymen were armed with infantry rifles and M1833 French short sabres. Shortly before the outbreak of the hostilities President Prado bought twelve additional Krupp mountain guns, but these were blockaded in Argentina and did not reach Peru until the end of the war. To face the growing need for new artillery pieces, by the end of 1879 the Peruvians started their own production of guns in Lima. The British John White supervised the production of the first eighty bronze guns (thirty-one mountain pieces and forty-nine field ones), which were local copies of the M1871 Vavasseur of 55mm (the Peruvians had some original Vavasseur guns mounted in the various fortifications of Lima). Despite being breech-loading and rifled, these "White" guns performed quite badly on the field of battle. In 1880 the Peruvian production continued under the direction of Juan Grieve, who produced thirty-two new guns that were local copies of the M1873 Krupp mountain gun of 6cm (as we have already seen the Peruvians had twelve original Krupp mountain guns in their arsenal). These "Grieve" guns were made with fused railroad tracks that were encased in bronze and reinforced with iron rings. As the "White" guns, they were breech-loading and rifled. During the battles for the defence of Lima, the Peruvians dismounted all the available guns from the fortifications of Lima and from the warships anchored in the port of Callao, using them as normal field pieces that were positioned in the two defensive lines of Chorrillos and Miraflores. At Chorrillos, in particular, the following guns were employed by the Peruvian defenders: twenty-three Whites, thirty-two Grieves, nine original Vavasseurs, four Walgely steel pieces, one Armstrong and two small Selay-system cannons. The resistance forces of the Army of the Centre always had between eight and twelve guns: a certain number of these were "White" ones, while others were smoothbores dismounted from fortifications to be used as normal field pieces.

UNIFORMS

Since the first dress regulations of 1825, the Peruvian Army adopted uniforms that followed very closely the contemporary French models. Initially the Spanish influence remained quite clear, but over time French style became dominant[36]. This general trend was confirmed by the following dress regulations of 1827, 1830, 1835, 1839 and 1852. The dress regulations of 1839, promulgated after the dissolution of the Peru-Bolivian Confederation, were the first to adopt light blue as distinctive colour of the Peruvian infantry; those of 1852, instead, were the first to copy the military dress of Napoleon III's Imperial Army (for example with the adoption of the tunic instead of the coatee and of the characteristic trousers in "garance" red). On 16 May 1863 new dress regulations were promulgated, according to which the infantry uniform was as follows: black shako with yellow pompom, brass decorative plate on the front (consisting of crossed laurel-and-palm branches) and Peruvian national cockade. Dark blue single-breasted tunic with light blue piping

35 Sater, William F., *Andean Tragedy: Fighting the War of the Pacific 1879–1884*, University of Nebraska, 2007
36 Ejército del Peru, *Evolucion Historica de los Uniformes del Ejercito del Peru (1821-1980)*, Lima, Peru, 2005

to collar, round cuffs and front. Golden contre-epaulettes and brass buttons. "Garance" red trousers with light blue piping; black gaiters (white during summer) and shoes. On campaign the shako was replaced by an entirely dark blue kepi with brass unit number on the front and the tunic was substituted with a shorter jacket having brass unit number on collar and no contre-epaulettes (piped in light blue to collar, round cuffs and front). The elite "Zepita" Battalion was the only one to have red kepis with dark blue bottom band. In general terms this uniform was extremely "French" and the Peruvian soldiers were very proud of it.

In 1870, however, the French Army was resoundingly defeated by the Prussians: this event had a great influence in South America, marking the beginning of the Prussian influence over the uniforms of that continent's military forces. The Peruvian government was the first in Latin America that decided to abandon French military fashions: according to its view, the brave Peruvian soldiers could not be dressed with the uniforms of a defeated army. This happened under the government of President Pardo, who was in the delicate process of reforming the army: as a result, in 1872 new dress regulations following Prussian style were promulgated. According to these, the new infantry uniform was as follows: "Pickelhaube" (spiked helmet) with brass frontal plate representing the Peruvian national shield; grey jacket with light blue piping to collar, rounded cuffs and front. Brass buttons and unit number on collar. Grey trousers with light blue piping, black shoes. In the following years and decades practically all South American armies followed the Peruvian example and substituted their French uniforms with new ones of Prussian cut. The Peruvian officers and soldiers, however, were proud of their previous uniforms and had no intention to abandon them: a public petition was sent to the government by the officers of the army, who requested permission to retain their French uniforms with "garance" trousers. The government, fearing negative reactions, agreed to the requests of the officer corps. This same problem remained for the enlisted men, with the result that at the outbreak of the hostilities in 1879 the majority of the Peruvian infantry was still dressed in the M1863 uniform (in its campaign version with kepi and jacket). The grey M1872 uniform was worn by very few soldiers and by not a single officer.

During the years between 1872 and 1879, the "garance" trousers of the M1863 uniform for rankers were generally substituted with new dark blue ones having light blue piping; some soldiers, however, preferred to replace them with the grey ones of the new M1872 uniform. The jacket of the M1863 uniform was slightly modified during this period: it often had light blue pointed cuffs instead of dark blue round ones. As a result of this very confused situation, the Peruvian infantrymen of 1879 presented a quite motley appearance: some had the M1863 dress with "garance" trousers; others had the M1863 jacket but dark blue or M1872 grey trousers; a few had the new M1872 uniform with "Pickelhaube". Rank was shown by inverted "chevrons", which were red for corporals and yellow for sergeants. The typical helmets worn with the grey uniform were bought from Germany and were Prussian M1867; amazingly, at the beginning of the war some of them had not yet been modified and still carried the German Imperial eagle as frontal plate. As an alternative to the kepi, Peruvian infantrymen could wear a simple fatigue cap patterned after the contemporary French "bonnet de police"; this was locally known as "cristina" or "coscacho" and could be in different colours: dark blue with white pompom and piping or white with red pompom and light blue piping.

Until 1878 Peru imported all the cloth needed for military uniforms from European countries (France in particular); in that year the situation changed, because the government of President Prado decided to start using cloth produced by Peruvian manufacturers in order to reduce the expenses for production of uniforms and help the national textile industry[37]. It was also determined, however, that clothing for parade uniforms was still to be bought from foreign producers (because of the lower quality of Peruvian cloth, acceptable

---

37 Greve-Moller P., Fernàndez-Cerda C., *Uniformes de la Guerra del Pacifico 1879-1884*, Santiago, Chile, 2008

only for campaign use). In April 1879 a General Supply Corps was created with the objective of uniforming the army on a more regular basis, but this did not achieve its goals and in January 1880 it was replaced by a Special Commission. The new administrative body, however, experienced the same problems of the Supply Corps and failed to achieve the required result of supplying the army. The basic campaign equipment of the Peruvian infantry consisted of just a few elements: a black leather waist belt with brass buckle, to which a black leather bayonet scabbard and cartridge pouch were attached; the former on the soldier's left flank and the latter on the back. A white canvas haversack and a round tin canteen with leather strap were universally carried. Like the Bolivian soldiers, Peruvian infantrymen carried a striped "poncho" wrapped around the waist: this was worn for protection against enemy bayonets and for making the use of the waist belt more comfortable. During night it was a perfect protection against cold of the Atacama Desert. The cartridge pouch could also be worn on the front of the waist belt, usually on the left side. As the war progressed, leather cartridge pouches gradually deteriorated due to the dry and salty environmental conditions in which the conflict was fought: as a result, they were replaced by new canvas cartridge belts made by the same soldiers (named "cananas") or by long ammunition bags (also made of canvas and known as "talegas"). Shoes and gaiters were not extremely popular, since most of the Peruvian soldiers were accustomed to walk for miles and miles barefoot. Bullhide sandals (known as "ojotas") were sometimes worn instead of shoes. Corks were generally used to protect the muzzle of rifles from dust; covers designed to preserve the delicate mechanisms of the weapons were also very popular.

OFFICERS

The standard uniform for Peruvian infantry and artillery officers consisted of a dark blue kepi with light blue bottom band (red with dark blue bottom band for artillery), piped in gold according to rank and with golden unit number on the front (a gold flaming grenade for artillery). A dark blue double-breasted tunic with golden buttons; collar, pointed cuffs and piping to the front were in the distinctive colours of infantry or artillery (respectively light blue or red). Rank was shown by gold inverted "chevrons" on the cuffs, worn together with gold epaulettes/contre-epaulettes or shoulder bars. Pointed cuffs became quite popular after 1872, but many officers still had tunics with dark blue round ones piped in light blue or red. Collars were generally plain, but many officers had them decorated with various kinds of golden embroidery (frequently patterned after branches of palm for the infantry and flaming grenades for the artillery). High ranking officers usually had golden piping on their trousers and additional gold embroidery also to cuffs. As an alternative to the double-breasted tunic, officers could also wear a single-breasted frock-coat with collar, pointed cuffs and frontal piping in the distinctive colour of their branch of service. Trousers could be "garance" red (piped in light blue for infantry and black for artillery) or the M1872 grey ones (piped in light blue for infantry and red for artillery). As we have already said, red trousers were dominant; with the progression of the hostilities, however, dark blue ones piped in light blue or red became quite popular. White trousers (sometimes piped in the distinctive colours of infantry and artillery) were universally worn during summer, together with white protective covers for the kepi (which usually had a neck curtain). On parade, golden gorgets were usually worn and the kepi was substituted with a low streamlined model of shako known as "ros" and copied from the Spanish Army; this existed in many non-regulated versions, but generally had a light blue or red plume and golden unit badges on the front (an Inca sun for infantry and a flaming grenade for artillery). On parade, artillery officers also wore additional golden cords and flounders. Apparently, a small number of Peruvian officers (especially from the artillery) wore the "Pickelhaube" helmet as parade headgear.

INFANTRY UNIFORMS OF THE FIRST AND SECOND CAMPAIGN

During the military campaigns of 1879 and 1880 Peruvian infantrymen, be they regulars or National Guardsmen, used two simple but practical uniforms: an entirely dark blue one for winter and an entirely white one for summer. The first was worn in the central and northern parts of the country; the second was worn during all seasons in the southern regions (where the conflict was effectively fought). We should bear in mind that the first two campaigns of the war were conducted in the Desert of Atacama, a very arid region where temperatures were extremely hot during the day and freezing at night. For this reason, soldiers needed tropical uniforms of light cloth as well as heavy greatcoats; the Peruvian government was able to supply its men with the formers but generally failed to produce a sufficient number of the latter. The winter uniform was as follows: dark blue kepi with brass unit number on the front; dark blue single-breasted jacket with brass unit number on collar; dark blue trousers and black shoes. The summer uniform was very simple: white kepi (usually with neck curtain), white single-breasted jacket, white trousers and black shoes. Both uniforms could have light blue piping to collar, round cuffs and front of the jacket. Rank was shown by the usual inverted "chevrons", but light blue for both corporals and sergeants. The trousers could also be piped in light blue. Apparently, some units continued to wear "garance" trousers piped in light blue with the winter uniform, but these were by no means practical for use on campaign. Headgears were quite varied: white havelocks could be worn with the dark blue kepi, while some units used the winter kepi also with the summer uniform. The "bonnet de police" remained as an alternative for use on campaign, but it was never popular as the kepi. Initially the Peruvian Army was not prepared for a war fought in a tropical environment and thus the first months of fighting were characterised by serious hardships for the common soldiers; in November 1879, however, 13,500 white canvas uniforms were finally produced and later distributed to all the men of the "Ejército del Sur". Summer uniforms were also largely produced with rag fabric (locally known as "bayeta"), which was less expensive and more resistant than canvas (locally named "loneta")[38]. Kerchiefs were frequently worn around the neck, as protection against sandstorms and to dry perspiration. A certain number of Peruvian infantry units, however, wore distinctive uniforms during the first two campaigns of the war:

5th Line Infantry Battalion "Cazadores del Cuzco": dark blue kepi with green bottom band and brass "chasseur" horn on the front. Dark blue double-breasted jacket with brass buttons; green collar and pointed cuffs. Brass "chasseur" horns on the collar. White trousers and black shoes.

15th Line Infantry Battalion "Cazadores del Misti": entirely green kepi with brass "chasseur" horn on the front. White single-breasted jacket with brass buttons; green collar and round cuffs. Brass "chasseur" horns on the collar. White trousers and black shoes.

17th Line Infantry Battalion "Guardias de Arequipa": entirely dark blue kepi with brass unit badge (a letter "G") on the front. Black single-breasted jacket with brass buttons; dark blue collar with brass unit badge. Red trousers and black shoes. It is interesting to note that black was the distinctive colour of all Peruvian police forces: when many of these were transformed into infantry units, they generally retained their peculiar black jackets.

19th Line Infantry Battalion "Granaderos del Cuzco": entirely white kepi. White single-breasted jacket with brass buttons; red collar and pointed cuffs. Brass flaming grenades on the collar. White trousers and black shoes.

National Guard Infantry Battalion "Cazadores de Piérola": white kepi with red bottom band and brass

38 Ejército del Peru, *Evolucion Historica de los Uniformes del Ejercito del Peru (1821-1980)*, Lima, Peru, 2005

73

"chasseur" horn on the front. White single-breasted jacket with brass buttons; red collar and round cuffs. Brass "chasseur" horns on the collar. Red trousers and black shoes.

National Guard Infantry Battalion "Vengadores de Grau": entirely dark blue kepi. Red single-breasted jacket with brass buttons; light blue collar, pointed cuffs and piping to the front. White trousers piped in light blue and black shoes.

INFANTRY UNIFORMS OF THE THIRD CAMPAIGN

After the disastrous Battle of Tacna, the few surviving units of the Peruvian Army returned to Lima in rags and practically without any kind of organization. President Piérola had to build up two new armies practically from zero and this incredible effort included also the provision of adequate uniforms and equipment to the new units. To achieve some degree of uniformity and to supply with proper military dress the newly-formed Army of the Reserve, Piérola ordered the promulgation of a new set of dress regulations on 12 July 1880. These detailed the uniforms that were to be worn by the new Army of the Reserve only, since the Army of the Line had to continue using the old models of uniforms worn during the first two war campaigns. The new uniforms issued by Piérola were elegant but simple, being intended for a practical use[39].

Officers: dark blue kepi with red quarter-piping and white metal unit number on the front. Dark blue double-breasted frock-coat or jacket with white metal buttons. White piping to dark blue round cuffs and front of the frock-coat/jacket. Golden shoulder bars. Dark blue trousers with white piping. Black shoes, frequently worn with white spats. The round cuffs could be simple or have an additional band of red piping.

Soldiers: the parade headgear consisted of a low black shako with brass unit number on the front and two thin lines of red piping (one on the top and one on the bottom). This frequently had a white havelock. Curiously this new and simple model of shako was rarely worn by units from the Army of the Reserve, while it became extremely popular among units of the Army of the Line (being worn as standard headgear also on campaign). The campaign headgear of the reserve units was very simple: an entirely dark blue kepi with white metal unit number on the front. The uniform consisted of a dark blue single-breasted or double-breasted jacket, which sometimes had white piping to collar, round cuffs, front and bottom edges. Rank was shown by the usual inverted "chevrons", light blue for corporals and yellow for sergeants. Buttons could be brass or white metal. Trousers could be entirely dark blue or have white piping. The black shoes were frequently worn with white gaiters.

The infantry of the Army of the Line continued to wear the previous uniforms used during the first two war campaigns, albeit with the introduction of the new shako as a possible alternative to the kepi. As always, some units wore distinctive uniforms, especially those formed specifically for the defence of Lima:

83rd Line Infantry Battalion "Ayacucho": this unit was formed by Colonel Miota together with the cavalry "Morochucos de la Muerte" and its men had the same ethnic origin of the more famous "gauchos" (being of mixed Indian and Spanish descent). This infantry battalion spent a month of training in Ayacucho before going to Lima in November 1880 together with the "Morochucos". The soldiers of this unit had a very peculiar uniform, different from the usual one worn by all the other infantry units of the Army of the Line: entirely black kepi with brass unit number on the front. Black single-breasted jacket with brass buttons and light blue piping on the collar, front and round cuffs. Black trousers with light blue piping and black shoes. These uniforms had been made by the women of Ayacucho with coarse fabric and had a large

---

39 Greve-Moller P., Fernàndez-Cerda C., *Uniforms of the Pacific War 1879-1884*, Nottingham, 2010

Inca sun embroidered in gold on the back of the jacket[40]. Apparently this symbol had a special meaning for the religious traditions of the Andean peoples and thus was worn as a sort of "protection" for soldiers.

National Guard Infantry Battalion "Guarnición de Marina": the soldiers of this elite unit had a very distinctive and elegant uniform, while the officers were dressed as their equivalents of the Peruvian Navy (with uniforms copied from the contemporary dress regulations of the Royal Navy). This battalion, in fact, was a mix between a line infantry unit and a naval infantry one. The uniform of officers was as follows: dark blue peaked cap with golden chinstrap, piping (according to rank) and naval emblem on the front (consisting of the Peruvian national shield over two crossed anchors). Dark blue double-breasted frock-coat with golden buttons and dark blue step collar. Golden epaulettes/contre-epaulettes (according to rank) and rank rings around the cuffs. White shirt and black bow tie. Dark blue trousers with large golden side-stripes and black short boots. The uniform of rankers was completely different: dark blue shako with golden chinstrap, having the same golden naval emblem of officers on the front and a pompom (half white and half red, divided vertically) sustained by a golden button. Dark blue tunic with red collar, pointed cuffs and frontal piping. White metal buttons, golden shoulder bars with a decorative anchor. The collar had dark blue patches bearing a golden anchor. White trousers piped in red, white gaiters and black shoes.

Soldier, National Guard Infantry Battalion "Guarnición de Marina". Drawing by Benedetto Esposito.

"Columna Policía de Seguridad de Lima": the policemen of Lima, as all the other Peruvian ones, were dressed in black. Their uniform was quite simple: entirely black kepi with white metal unit badge on the front (depicting the heraldic shield of Lima). Entirely black single-breasted frock-coat with brass buttons; entirely black trousers and shoes.

"Guardia Urbana": the foreign firemen of Lima who formed the Urban Guard during the emergency that followed the Battle of Miraflores were dressed with the typical uniform of Peruvian "bomberos". This consisted of black or dark blue kepi, bearing on the front a red patch with the company's name written in gold. Black single-breasted jacket with brass buttons, red trousers and tall black boots (typical of firemen).

INFANTRY UNIFORMS OF THE FOURTH CAMPAIGN

Cáceres tried to dress the infantry battalions of his Army of the Centre in the most possible "regular" way, but his forces never achieved any degree of uniformity regarding dress. Especially during the first months of guerrilla operations against the Chileans, Cáceres' men were mostly dressed with their civilian clothing (the traditional costume of the Quechua Indians), with the exception of the few ex-regulars who probably continued to wear their old uniforms. To distinguish his men in some way, Cáceres ordered them to put a stripe of red cloth on their civilian headgear: this practice soon made red the distinctive colour of

---

40 Greve-Moller P., Fernàndez-Cerda C., *Uniformes de la Guerra del Pacifico 1879-1884*, Santiago, Chile, 2008

Officers of the 2nd Line Infantry Battalion "Zepita" in 1879, wearing M1863 service dress.

the resistance forces operating under Cáceres' guidance[41]. As the war progressed, the regular units of the Army of the Centre gradually adopted a red kepi as universal headgear: this could have a white curtain for protection of the neck and was sometimes worn also by the irregular groups of Quechua "guerrilleros". With the few funds at his disposal Cáceres tried to dress his battalions with coarse cotton cloth (locally known as "tocuyo asargado") in sea green colour. However, due to the chronic economic restrictions, only the 5th Infantry Battalion "Canta" (initially named "Huancayo") received this new uniform. The other battalions wore uniforms of coarse cotton cloth in white or, more rarely, in grey. These were very simple and generally had no decorative details, being produced and woven by the Quechua women. The voluntary contribution from the small mountain villages of central Peru was very important to dress and equip Cáceres' forces.

1st Infantry Battalion "Tarapacá": white kepi with red bottom band and brass unit number on the front. White single-breasted jacket with red collar and pointed cuffs. Brass buttons. White trousers.

41 Ejército del Peru, *Evolucion Historica de los Uniformes del Ejercito del Peru (1821-1980)*, Lima, Peru, 2005

2nd Infantry Battalion "Zepita": grey kepi with red bottom band and brass unit number on the front. Grey single-breasted jacket with red collar and pointed cuffs. Brass buttons. Grey trousers. Later this battalion changed uniform and adopted a new white one that was exactly as that worn by the "Tarapacá" Battalion.

5th Infantry Battalion "Huancayo": entirely red kepi with brass unit badge on the front (an Inca sun). Sea green single-breasted jacket with red collar and pointed cuffs. Brass buttons. Sea green trousers. When the unit changed name to "Canta" it received a new grey uniform that was exactly as that worn by the "Zepita" Battalion.

Officers tended to use what uniforms they already had or could buy, but over time a certain degree of uniformity was achieved. The standard uniform of the officers from the Army of the Centre was as follows: dark blue kepi with red bottom band, golden unit badge on the front (an Inca sun) and golden quarter-piping (according to rank). Dark blue double-breasted frock-coat with red collar and pointed cuffs. Brass buttons, golden shoulder bars and inverted "chevrons" on cuffs (according to rank). White trousers with large red side-stripes and black shoes or boots.

The infantrymen of Iglesias' Army of the North initially had no uniform, being dressed with simple white jackets (having brass buttons) and trousers. To differentiate his men from those of Cáceres' Army, Iglesias ordered them to wear an entirely dark blue kepi with brass unit number on the front. This was the only item of dress worn by all the soldiers of the Army of the North. When this transformed itself into the new "Regenerating Army", Iglesias started to receive formal assistance by the Chileans in order to organize his forces on a more regular basis. As a result, the Chilean General Supply Corps sold uniforms and equipment to the Army of the North

Lieutenant of the 2nd Line Infantry Battalion "Zepita", wearing M1863 service dress. Drawing by Benedetto Esposito.

at very good conditions and prices. Iglesias, however, had also been able to conclude a contract with the Grace Brothers Company in the USA for the acquisition of surplus campaign uniforms from the stores of the Unionist Army (surplus from the US Civil War). As a result, the 1st Line Infantry Battalion "Regenerador" received uniforms supplied by the Chileans and the 2nd Line Infantry Battalion "Cajamarca" wore the American ones bought from the Grace Brothers Company. In any case Iglesias' infantrymen retained their dark blue kepis with brass unit number of the front: these remained distinctive of the Army of the North also during the subsequent civil war against Cáceres' forces (which continued to use their red kepis).

1st Line Infantry Battalion "Regenerador": dark blue kepi with brass unit number on the front. Light blue-grey double-breasted jacket with red collar and round cuffs. Brass buttons, red trousers and buff leather boots.

2nd Line Infantry Battalion "Cajamarca": dark blue kepi with brass unit number on the front. Entirely dark blue single-breasted jacket with brass buttons. Light blue trousers, white spats and black shoes.

CAVALRY

Unluckily the information that we have about Peruvian cavalry uniforms is quite scarce: at the beginning of the war in 1879 it seems that the three cavalry units ("Húsares de Junín", "Lanceros de Torata" and "Guías") used different uniforms. The Hussars were still dressed with M1863 "French" uniforms, while the Lancers had adopted the new "Prussian" dress prescribed for cavalry by the new M1872 dress regulations. We don't know if the Guides had adopted the new Prussian uniform or if they still wore the old French one.

1st Line Cavalry Regiment "Húsares de Junín": red kepi with dark blue bottom band and piping, with brass unit badge on the front (an Inca sun) and white neck protector. Dark blue single-breasted jacket with red collar and brass buttons. Red piping to round cuffs and front. Red trousers with double side-stripes and black leather boots. Officers were dressed very similarly but had golden piping on the kepi and golden shoulder bars. In addition their cuffs were pointed and the sleeves of their jackets were decorated with golden Hungarian knots[42]. The "Húsares de Junín" Regiment fought valiantly during the first two campaigns of the conflict, demonstrating to be the best mounted unit deployed by the Peruvians. This regiment, no doubt one of the most important in the history of the Peruvian Army, was formed in 1821 during the campaign for the liberation of Peru guided by San Martín. It fought particularly well during the important battle of Junín (1824) and, for this reason, received its famous name from the same Bolívar. In the following decades the Hussars took part to all the wars which saw Peruvian involvement, always demonstrating their valour.

Soldier, 2nd Line Infantry Battalion "Cajamarca" from Iglesias' Army of the North. Drawing by Benedetto Esposito.

2nd Line Cavalry Regiment "Lanceros de Torata": "Pickelhaube" (spiked helmet) with brass frontal plate representing the Peruvian national shield and Peruvian national cockade. Dark blue single-breasted coatee with red piping to collar, pointed cuffs, frontal and bottom edges. Brass buttons. The collar bore a brass unit badge, consisting of crossed palm-and-sabre. Dark blue trousers with red piping and black leather boots. Officers had golden shoulder boards.

Regarding the National Guard cavalry units formed during the first two war campaigns, we have details only for two of them:

42 Greve-Moller P., Fernàndez-Cerda C., *Uniforms of the Pacific War 1879-1884*, Nottingham, 2010

*Soldier of the 2nd Line Cavalry Regiment
"Lanceros de Torata", wearing M1872
uniform. Drawing by Benedetto Esposito.*

*Trooper, National Guard Cavalry
Column "Gendarmes de Tacna".
Drawing by Benedetto Esposito.*

National Guard Cavalry Squadron "Lanceros de Tacna": dark blue kepi with red bottom band and piping, with brass unit badge on the front (crossed palm-and-sabre). Dark blue double-breasted tunic with red collar and pointed cuffs. Brass buttons, same brass badge of the kepi also on the collar. Red trousers with dark blue piping, black leather boots. Officers had golden piping on the kepi, golden shoulder bars and gold Hungarian knots on the sleeves of the tunic.

National Guard Cavalry Column "Columna Gendarmes de Tacna": these ex-policemen from the city of Tacna wore a very simple but elegant uniform. Straw hat with red band; dark blue double-breasted tunic with light blue collar and pointed cuffs. Brass buttons and unit badge on the collar (presumably the heraldic shield of Tacna). Red trousers with dark blue piping, black leather boots. Officers had golden shoulder bars, inverted "chevrons" on the cuffs and piping to trousers.

Regarding the National Guard cavalry units formed for the defence of Lima, we have details only for two of them:

National Guard Cavalry Regiment "Cazadores del Rímac": red kepi with a light blue bottom band and piping, having brass unit badge on the front (a "chasseur" horn). Dark blue single-breasted jacket with light blue collar, pointed cuffs and piping to the front. Brass buttons. Red trousers with light blue piping and black leather boots. This cavalry unit had a very peculiar history: on 23 July 1879 the Chilean transport ship "Rímac" was captured by the Peruvians near the port of Antofagasta. In that moment it was transporting the 1st Squadron of the "Carabineros de Yungay", with a total of 258 men and 215 horses plus a great quantity of weapons, ammunitions and equipment. With this large amount of captured material, on 26 March 1880 the Peruvians formed the new cavalry regiment "Cazadores del Rímac", which derived its name from the captured ship. The soldiers of this unit received the excellent horses, weapons and uniforms of the "Carabineros de Yungay"[43]: the only difference from the original Chilean dress was the brass unit badge on the kepi. Weapons consisted of M1866 Winchester carbines and old M1796 British light cavalry sabres, as used by the Chilean cavalry. The new Peruvian regiment had two squadrons: one was of mounted fusiliers and the other of lancers (having lances with pennants in the Peruvian national colours of red and white). The "Cazadores del Rímac", however, were quite short-lived: the unit was completely annihilated at the Battle of El Manzano on 27 December 1880.

Gunner, Artillery Brigade of the Reserve, battles for the defence of Lima. Drawing by Benedetto Esposito.

National Guard Cavalry Regiment "Morochucos de la Muerte": the dress of the Morochucos was made by the women of Ayacucho, with a fabric called "jerga" of grey or black colour. They usually had slouch hats or fur caps. The most traditional element of their outfit was the colourful "poncho". Some of them had sabres, but the majority was armed only with lances. These had pennants in two different versions: red with white skull and crossbones or white with black skull and crossbones. The symbols on the pennants, like the unit's name, were ideated by their commander Colonel Miota.

ARTILLERY

At the beginning of the war Peruvian artillerymen were more or less in the same confused situation of infantry soldiers regarding uniforms: the majority of them were still wearing the old M1863 "French" uniform, while only a little number had adopted the new M1872 dress in Prussian style. The M1863 uniform was as follows: dark blue kepi with red piping and brass flaming grenade on the front. Dark blue double-breasted tunic with red piping to collar, pointed cuffs and front. Brass buttons and flaming grenades on collar. Red trousers with black piping, black shoes. The M1872 uniform was very similar to that of cavalry: "Pickelhaube" (spiked helmet) with brass frontal plate showing two crossed cannons and Peruvian national cockade. Dark blue single-breasted coatee with red collar,

43 Greve-Moller P., Fernàndez-Cerda C., *Uniformes de la Guerra del Pacifico 1879-1884*, Santiago, Chile, 2008

round cuffs and piping to frontal and bottom edges. Brass buttons. The collar bore brass flaming grenades. Dark blue trousers with red piping and black shoes. Once on the southern front, Peruvian artillerymen received the same entirely white summer/tropical uniforms worn by the infantry: white single-breasted jacket with brass buttons, white trousers and black shoes. These could have red piping to collar, round cuffs, front and trousers. Headgear consisted of a dark blue kepi with a brass unit badge on the front (two crossed cannons under a flaming grenade). The new dress regulations of 12 July 1880 prescribed the following simple uniform for artillery soldiers of the Army of the Reserve: light blue-grey kepi with red flaming grenade on the front, light blue-grey single-breasted jacket with red collar and piping to front and pointed cuffs. Light blue-grey trousers with red piping, white gaiters and black shoes. The artillerymen of Cáceres' Army of the Centre were dressed very simply: white kepi with red bottom band and brass unit badge on the front (two crossed cannons under a flaming grenade). White single-breasted jacket with red collar and pointed cuffs. Brass buttons, white trousers and black shoes.

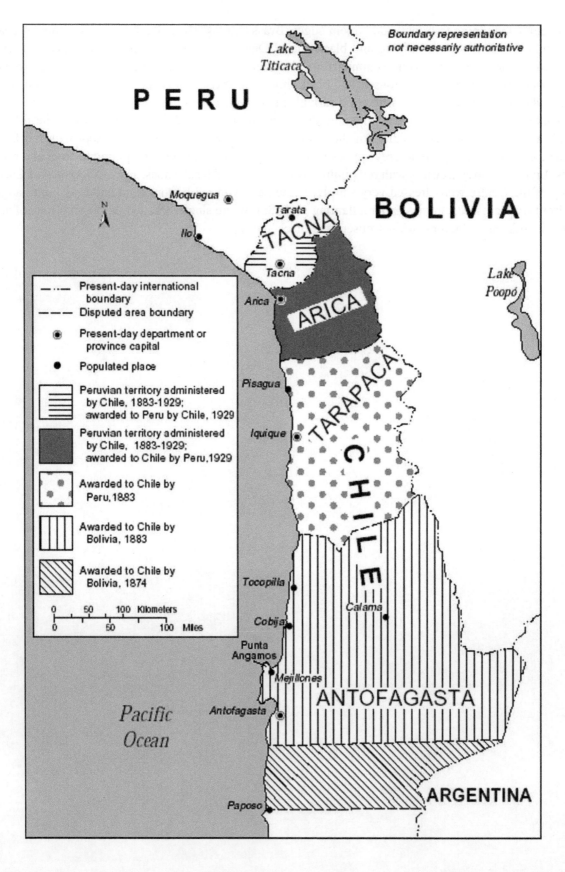

Aníbal Pinto Garmendia, President of Chile during 1876-1881.

THE CHILEAN ARMY

ORGANIZATION

After achieving formal independence from Spain in 1818, Chile played an important role in the last and decisive campaigns fought by the new South American countries against the remaining military forces of the Spanish Empire. The last Chilean operations against Spanish strongholds were conducted as late as 1826. The first years of the new republic, however, saw the outbreak of a bloody civil war in 1829: this lasted until April 1830 and saw the clash between Liberals and Conservatives for political domination over the new independent country. In the end the Conservative party was able to defeat the Liberals and gradually brought all the rebel provinces under control of the central government. After the civil war all the units that had sided with the Liberals were disbanded and a new organization of the army was made effective. According to this, the Chilean Army was to be structured on four infantry battalions, two regiments and one squadron of cavalry, six companies of artillery. The two cavalry regiments were one of "Cazadores a Caballo" (Mounted Chasseurs) and one of "Granaderos a Caballo" (Mounted Grenadiers), while the single squadron was of Hussars. In April 1832 the cavalry was enlarged with the creation of a new independent company, which had to serve on Chile's southern frontier against the incursions of the local Indians. This new corps was known as "Carabineros de la Frontera" (Carabineers of the Frontier). In August of 1832 one of the four infantry battalions was disbanded. Since its formation the Chilean Army also included a small corps of engineer officers: like many other South American countries Chile did not have separate units of Engineers, but just a staff of officers having engineering competence. As clear from the above description, the Chilean Army was a small force that was distributed across a very large national territory.

According to the Constitution of 1823, the Chilean Army could count on the support of a general militia, known as "Milicia Civica": this, however, initially existed only on paper[44]. Since 1830 this situation started to change, because the militia underwent a progressive but radical reorganization and adopted the new denomination of "Guardia Civica". All able-bodied men aged between 14 and 50 had to serve in it, paying for their own uniforms. The new planned organization initially achieved success only in the capital of Chile, Santiago, where four battalions of infantry and an artillery brigade with two companies were formed. As time progressed, however, new units of the Civic Guard started to be formed also in some other Chilean cities: by 1835 these included fourteen battalions and three companies of infantry; three regiments, sixteen squadrons and one company of cavalry; three brigades and one company of artillery (for a total of 4,500 men). Training was made once a week (on Sunday) and the general level of the units became soon quite good. In contrast to other South American countries, where the National Guard was usually neglected and badly organized, Chile counted on a well-trained auxiliary corps that could function as a source of manpower for the regular army in case of war. This way the small regular forces could be easily and rapidly enlarged with the inclusion of new recruits coming from the units of the National Guard, men already

44 Estado Mayor General del Ejercito, *Historia del Ejercito de Chile*, Santiago, Chile, 1980-1983

having some sort of military training and knowledge. In addition, the Chilean National Guard was intended since its foundation as an important element in the hands of politicians to contrast the power of the military elites: the National Guard acted as a barrier of defence against any attempt of military coup, balancing the role of military officers in Chilean politics. During the following wars against external enemies, the National Guard would also mobilize entire units for service on the front at the side of the regulars.

In 1836, at the outbreak of the war against the Peru-Bolivian Confederation, the Chilean regular military forces comprised the following units: three battalions of infantry (each with four companies of fusiliers, one of grenadiers and one of chasseurs), two regiments of cavalry (each having three squadrons of two companies), one squadron of Hussars, one company of Carabineers and one regiment of artillery (with six companies, one of which was mounted). In total 3,000 men, to which 4,500 men of the Civic Guard could be added. It became soon clear to the Chilean high command that the army had to be enlarged in order to face the massive menace coming from the joint forces of Peru and Bolivia. The best of the three infantry battalions, the "Cazadores de Maipo", was expanded and transformed into a regiment with two battalions. The "Carabineros de la Frontera" were transformed into a squadron with two companies, while the Mounted Grenadiers Regiment was augmented with the addition of a fourth squadron (made up of lancers and acting as a sort of semi-independent unit). Shortly before the departure of the first Chilean expedition against the Peru-Bolivian Confederation, the "Cazadores de Maipo" mutinied and tried to launch a revolution against the government. The revolutionary movement failed and the "Cazadores de Maipo" Regiment was officially disbanded; as replacements for the dissolved unit, two new infantry battalions were formed: these were named "Portales" and "Valparaiso". The Civic Guard, by now commonly known as National Guard, contributed to the war effort with the mobilization of six infantry battalions: "Aconcagua", "Valparaiso", "Colchagua", "Santiago", "Chillán" and "Talca". During the conflict, the organization of the army saw only some minor modifications, like the creation of a provisional cavalry company of Guides (which had to serve with the army on the field). After the end of the war the six battalions of National Guard infantry were disbanded, together with the company of Guides, the extra squadron of the "Granaderos a Caballo" and the "Carabineros de la Frontera".

Chilean officer wearing campaign dress and equipment, including a traditional "corvo".

In 1844 the squadron of Hussars, which acted as presidential mounted escort, was disbanded and substituted with a new squadron of Cuirassiers having the same purposes. The life of this new unit was very short and confused: it soon changed denomination (becoming a

86

squadron of Guides) and in 1845 it was dissolved. The functions of presidential escort were now to be performed by the 1st Squadron of the Mounted Grenadiers Regiment. In that same year the following modifications were made to the organization of the army: the infantry battalions were reduced from four to three, while the "Granaderos a Caballo" Regiment had just two squadrons instead of three. The number of infantry battalions, however, was soon augmented again to four. In 1845 the National Guard was formally put under control of the regular army, which officers started to have a more active role in the training of National Guardsmen and began to conduct formal inspections on a regular basis. After a new civil war in 1851, the Chilean Army was again reorganized during the following year. According to the new structure, it was to comprise the following units: 5 battalions of infantry, two regiments of cavalry (Mounted Grenadiers and Mounted Chasseurs), one independent squadron of cavalry (the "Lanceros de Colchagua") and one regiment of artillery (with six, foot companies and two horse ones). In 1853 the infantry battalions were again reduced to four. In 1856 the Squadron of Lancers was disbanded. Another civil war took place during 1859, leading to the formation of several new units for service against the insurgents: at this time, however, the various provisional corps were disbanded as soon as the war ended. After the demobilization following the campaign of 1859, the Chilean Army was structured as follows: six infantry battalions, two cavalry regiments, one independent cavalry squadron (the "Carabineros de los Andes") and one regiment of artillery (on three brigades). The new squadron of Carabineers (formed during the war) was disbanded very soon; the number of infantry battalions was again reduced to five in 1860. During the Chincha Islands War the number of infantry units was increased as part of the temporary measures intended to enlarge the army, but as soon as the Spanish menace vanished the Chilean military forces went back to their previous organization[45].

The Chilean General Staff; note the use of white tropical pith helmets made of cork.

45 Peri-Fagerstrom, René, *Los Batallones Bulnes y Valparaiso en la Guerra del Pacifico*, Santiago, Chile, 1980

During the war against the Peru-Bolivian Confederation, the commanders of the Chilean Navy felt an increasing need for some units of naval infantry: as a result, after the end of the conflict, a first independent company of naval infantry was formed in Valparaiso on 14 April 1840. The soldiers of this unit not only acted as marines, but also as garrison troops for the land bases of the navy (Valparaiso and Punta Arenas). In 1841 the company of naval infantry was replaced by five little squads of marines, each numbering just one sergeant, one corporal and ten soldiers. On 9 May 1843 the Chilean naval infantry was reorganized again, this time on a more solid base: now it was structured on a brigade with two companies. Since its formation, the naval infantry was considered as an elite unit, taking part in all the military campaigns that saw the involvement of the Chilean forces. On 26 September 1865 the Naval Infantry Brigade was transformed into a battalion with 800 men. During this period the Chilean marines received additional training as naval artillerymen and thus performed extremely well while embarked on warships during the Chincha Islands War against Spain. As a result, on 4 August 1866, the Naval Infantry Battalion changed its name to Naval Artillery Battalion; according to the new statute, the unit was under control of the Navy when serving on warships or in naval bases and under control of the Army when serving on land. From an administrative point of view, however, it was part of the Navy. The battalion was now to comprise six companies with 120 men each and had a certain number of bronze naval guns; this structure was maintained with no changes until the beginning of the War of the Pacific in 1879.

THE CHILEAN ARMY AT THE BEGINNING OF THE WAR

According to the decree of 12 September 1878, the Chilean regular forces numbered 3,122 men (including 401 officers, 100 of whom were assigned to the training of the National Guard) and comprised the following units:

- 1st Line Infantry Battalion "Buín"

- 2nd Line Infantry Battalion

- 3rd Line Infantry Battalion

- 4th Line Infantry Battalion

- Line Infantry Battalion "Zapadores de la Frontera"

- Line Cavalry Regiment "Granaderos a Caballo"

- Line Cavalry Regiment "Cazadores a Caballo"

- Line Artillery Regiment

- Naval Artillery Battalion

Emilio Sotomayor Baeza, one of the most important and experienced Chilean officers.

It is interesting to note that only the 1st Line Infantry Battalion, the best unit of the army, had a name; the other three battalions had only consecutive numbers and no further identification. Each of the four, line battalions had 300 men and the usual internal organization with six companies: four of fusiliers, one of grenadiers and one of "chasseurs". On 26 March 1879, during

Chilean Staff officers; in the background there are cavalrymen with M1852 parade dress.

the diplomatic crisis that led to the war with Peru and Bolivia, the four battalions were transformed into regiments with two battalions each; the new battalions were to have four companies each, for a total of thirty-two, line infantry companies. In addition, a new line infantry battalion had already been added to the army: on 26 March it received the same new organization of the other ones (being transformed into a regiment). This new unit was initially known as "Santiago" Regiment; only later in the war (on 26 October 1881, after the campaign of Lima) it received a progressive number, becoming the 5th Line Infantry Regiment[46]. The "Zapadores de la Frontera" had a very peculiar history: until 24 April 1877 they had been a battalion of the line infantry, but on that date, they were transformed into a new unit having a composite nature. Formally the battalion was still part of the line infantry, but now it was to perform new duties both as a frontier unit (deployed on the southern borders of Chile, to contrast the Indian incursions) and as an engineer corps ("zapadores" is the Spanish term for sappers). To sum up, they were a sort of combat engineers who could easily act both as normal infantry and as sappers. The "Zapadores de la Frontera" not only served on the frontier as garrison troops, but also as military colonists: their tasks included the colonization and the developing of agriculture on the Indian border of Chile. The soldiers of this unit had to build up bridges, open new ways of communication, patrol and manage the telegraphic lines, protect local hospitals and garrison military buildings located on the frontier. At the beginning of the war they numbered 300 men as the other four, line infantry battalions, organized into four companies; on 21 February 1879 they were augmented to six companies. With the outbreak of the hostilities, the battalion was transformed into a regiment structured on three brigades (each brigade having two companies). The Mounted Grenadiers Regiment had two squadrons with 100 men each, while the Mounted Chasseurs had three squadrons (always with 100 men each). On 29 March 1879 a fourth squadron was added to the "Cazadores a Caballo" Regiment; during the following May this additional squadron was used as the nucleus for the formation of a new line cavalry regiment, known as "Carabineros de Yungay" (with two squadrons). The Line Artillery

---

46 Sater, William F., *Andean Tragedy: Fighting the War of the Pacific 1879–1884*, University of Nebraska, 2007

Regiment was structured on two batteries/brigades, with two companies of 100 gunners each. Later it was expanded to eight companies instead of four, one of which was to be of mounted artillery. On 26 March 1879 the artillery detachment that was located in the city of Antofagasta (the 2nd Company of the 2nd Battery/Brigade) was transformed into an independent brigade with two companies, later expanded to become a new artillery battalion on 24 April. On 29 August 1879 the Artillery Battalion of Antofagasta was transformed into a regiment, which became the 2nd of the Line. This was initially structured on five brigades with two batteries each, one of which was to serve as a separate garrison unit to protect the coast of the newly-conquered areas. On 3 April 1879 the Naval Artillery Battalion was augmented to the strength of a regiment, with two battalions of four companies each (for a total of 1,200 men). At the beginning of the war the corps of engineer officers consisted of just twelve officers, who were too few to face the needs of the new conflict and who had no men under their direct command. As a result, on 6 June 1879, a first independent company of pontoniers was formed in Antofagasta. On 3 September 1879 this company was transformed into the new "Cuerpo de Ingenieros" (Engineer Corps), which included the corps of engineer officers and two companies of pontoniers.

THE NATIONAL GUARD

In 1871 the Chilean National Guard reached its numerical peak of 50,000 men, being the most remarkable organization of this kind at that time active in South America[47]. In 1876, however, Chile had to face a strong economic crisis that led to some significant cuts. The government, suffering from a great lack of funds, preferred to reduce the number of National Guard units instead of depriving the regular army of further resources (the regular units were already too few and too small). As a result, the number of National Guardsmen was reduced to 6,661 men, organized into the following units: three brigades, six battalions and one company of infantry (total 2,944 men); five squadrons of cavalry (total 1,288 men) and eight brigades of artillery (total 1,827 men). If compared to the joint military forces mobilized at the beginning

47 Estado Mayor General del Ejercito, *Historia del Ejercito de Chile*, Santiago, Chile, 1980-1983

Municipal Guardsmen from Santiago, wearing their pre-war uniforms in French style.

of the war by Peru and Bolivia, the number of Chilean soldiers seemed totally inadequate: less than 10,000 men, the majority of whom only had a superficial military training. The small expansion of the regular army that took place during the weeks before and after the declaration of war was obviously not enough to significantly enlarge the Chilean military forces: to face the emergency, the government decided to mobilize and expand the National Guard, preferring this more immediate measure to a further enlargement of the regulars. After all the basic organization and structure of the National Guard were very solid and only needed to be increased with a massive recruitment of new volunteers. This was exactly what happened, leading to an incredibly rapid expansion of the Chilean manpower available for the war that surprised the military leaders of Peru and Bolivia. Very soon new units of the National Guard started to be formed and mobilized in all the provinces of Chile, thanks to the great patriotic spirit of the population. The National Guard was now divided between "Guardia Nacional Movilizada" and "Guardia Nacional Estática": the former consisted of the units mobilized for war service together with the army, while the latter consisted of the units that remained of garrison in Chile (mostly taking the place of the regulars as garrison forces on the Indian frontier). Mobilized units had more or less the same training and weapons of the regulars and thus their general level was quite high. Here we will now give some basic information on the Mobilized National Guard units that took part to the military operations against Peru and Bolivia:

National Guard Infantry Battalions "Antofagasta", "Caracoles" and "Salinas": on 14 February 1879 the Chilean military forces occupied the Bolivian city of Antofagasta and its surroundings (including the coast), which were mostly inhabited by Chileans who lived and worked there as miners. As soon as Antofagasta was conquered, without meeting any opposition from the few Bolivian defenders, the Chilean authorities ordered the formation of two local National Guard battalions for protection of the newly-conquered areas. The local Chilean community responded very enthusiastically to this call: the two new units, each numbering 300 men, were soon formed and used to garrison the city and its surroundings. The flow of local volunteers wishing to serve in the National Guard was so strong that on 18 May 1879 two new battalions (the 3rd and 4th) were added to the garrison of Antofagasta. These new units had 300 men each. Later a National Guard cavalry squadron was also formed. Despite the initial enthusiasms, however, the National Guard battalions of Antofagasta played

Captain of the 1st National Guard Infantry Battalion "Antofagasta".

91

Soldier of the National Guard Infantry Regiment "Valparaiso", wearing M1880 campaign dress with divisional and unit marks. Note the canvas belts for carrying ammunitions.

no active role during the war (being always stationed in their city or being used as a source of replacements for the combat units). On 27 January 1880 the 1st, 3rd and 4th Battalions were disbanded together with the cavalry squadron; the remaining unit was transformed for a brief period into a regiment, but on 12 April 1880 it was again reduced to the strength of a battalion. The history of the "Caracoles" Battalion was very similar to that of the units formed in Antofagasta: created on 15 February 1879 in the important mining town of Caracoles, it served as a garrison unit defending the local mines until being disbanded on 30 March 1880. The "Salinas" Battalion was raised on 17 February 1879 in the settlement of Las Salinas, being composed by local Chilean miners as the other units. As the battalions formed in Antofagasta and Caracoles, it performed only garrison duties in the newly-occupied areas and did not play any active role in the military operations.

National Guard Infantry Battalions "Bulnes" and "Valparaiso": similarly, to what happened in Peru, a first and strong contribution to the formation of the National Guard came from the police forces of the major cities. In 1879 the city of Santiago had a strongly-militarized police corps structured on two sections, which numbered 715 men in total[48].The city of Valparaiso, the second largest one of Chile and the most important port of the country, had a Municipal Guard of 400 men distributed into four companies. In addition, there were also 800 non-militarized policemen, known as "celadores" and mainly operating for the security of the port. With the outbreak of the hostilities and the subsequent call for new units of the National Guard, the two cities of Santiago and Valparaiso decided to use a great part of their policemen in order to form new units for service against Peru and Bolivia. The generous offer of the two cities was immediately accepted by the central government, which authorised the creation of two National Guard battalions. Santiago formed the Battalion "Bulnes", with 500 policemen, on 12 April 1879; Valparaiso formed the Battalion "Valparaiso", with 600 Municipal Guardsmen and "celadores", on 9 April 1879. To perform the police functions needed to keep order in two large cities like Santiago and Valparaiso, the urban authorities decided to militarize the local companies of firemen ("bomberos") and gave them weapons. After a brief period of training in order to adapt to their new police duties, the firemen of the two cities were soon able to act as urban guards (something that they did until the return of policemen from the front). As for the firemen of Lima, those of Santiago and Valparaiso included many foreigners in their ranks. The "Valparaiso" Battalion returned to its home city after the Battle of Tacna, but it was soon replaced by a new unit having its same name (this time a regiment) that had already been formed as a replacement for the original battalion. This new "Valparaiso" Regiment was later disbanded after the Lima campaign and its men assembled with those of the "Navales" Battalion in order to form the new National Guard Infantry Battalion "Miraflores". The latter participated to the fourth campaign of the conflict, taking part to the last actions against the Peruvian resistance forces before being disbanded. The "Bulnes" Battalion, instead, fought also at Chorrillos and Miraflores before going back to Chile after the occupation of Lima. In Santiago, however, a new 2nd "Bulnes" Battalion had already been formed to replace the original unit; this was sent to Peru and took part to the fourth war campaign.

National Guard Infantry Battalion "Chacabuco": formed in Santiago on 26 April 1879, with 600 men on four companies. During the second war campaign it was augmented to six companies and took part with great valour to all the most important engagements[49]. On 2 August 1880, for the campaign of Lima, it was transformed into a regiment with two battalions (each having four companies). During the battles for Lima the "Chacabuco" again demonstrated to be one of the best National Guard units. In March-April 1881, as part of the general reorganization of the Chilean Army and National Guard, the "Chacabuco" Regiment was absorbed into the regular forces as the 6th Infantry Battalion of the Line and reduced to six companies.

---

48 Peri-Fagerstrom, René, *Los Batallones Bulnes y Valparaiso en la Guerra del Pacífico*, Santiago, Chile, 1980
49 Greve-Moller, Patricio, *Crónica del Chacabuco 6° de Línea*, Santiago, Chile, 2010

The "Chacabuco" at the beginning of the war, with grey greatcoats and Peruvian helmets.

Colonel of the National Guard Infantry Regiment "Chacabuco".

Captain of the National Guard Infantry Regiment "Chacabuco", in campaign dress.

Officers and soldiers of the National Guard Infantry Battalion "Navales".

National Guard Infantry Battalion "Navales": formed in Valparaiso on 29 April 1879 as "Civic Battalion of Naval Artillery", this unit had already existed during the Chincha Islands War against Spain (during which the port of Valparaiso had been heavily bombarded by the Spanish warships). This battalion was strongly influenced in its character and uniform by the regular Naval Artillery Battalion, but its soldiers (mostly ex-sailors and ex-longshoremen from the port of Valparaiso) were equipped and trained as normal infantry and depended only from the Army. At its formation the unit numbered 600 men, but by the time of the Lima campaign it had 800 men organized into six companies (being one of the largest National Guard battalions of the Chilean Army). On 10 November 1881 it was disbanded, and its men were melted with those of the "Valparaiso" Regiment in order to form the new National Guard Infantry Battalion "Miraflores".

National Guard Infantry Battalion "Cazadores del Desierto": organized in Santiago on 29 April 1879, with 600 men distributed into four companies. Despite being formed by Chileans, this unit was initially named "Foreign Legion" in imitation of the famous French corps. Only some officers actually came from Europe, most notably from Britain and France. Due to the strong protests of the French diplomats in Santiago, who wished to avoid any impression that France was supporting Chile in the conflict, the title of the battalion was changed to "Cazadores del Desierto" (Chasseurs of the Desert) on 14 May 1879. On that same day the unit was reorganized on two brigades of two companies each. On 14 August 1880, after taking part to the Battle of Tacna, the battalion was finally disbanded.

National Guard Infantry Battalion "Lautaro": formed on 2 May 1879 in Valparaiso; on 5 June it was transformed into a regiment having two battalions of 600 men each. Many of its men were Chileans who had returned to their home country due to the outbreak of the war. This unit took part to all the most important battles of the War of the Pacific (including Tacna, Chorrillos and Miraflores). Differently from the majority of the National Guard units, it was not disbanded after the occupation of Lima and fought also during the fourth campaign (albeit as a battalion and not as a regiment). It was finally dissolved only at the end of the conflict in 1884.

Lieutenant of the National Guard Infantry Regiment "Lautaro".

Soldier of the National Guard Infantry Regiment "Atacama".

National Guard Infantry Battalion "Atacama": formed on 13 May 1879 in Copiapó, mostly with miners from the region of Atacama. Initially the Chilean government had no intention to mobilize this National Guard unit for service on the front; in fact, it was decided to use 200 men from this battalion in order to complete the ranks of the 2nd Line Infantry Regiment. The provincial authorities of Copiapó, however, made strong pressures on the central government in order to obtain the mobilization of the "Atacama" Battalion; this objective was finally achieved on 30 June 1879. At this point of the war the battalion had four companies of 98 men each. The soldiers of the "Atacama" Battalion fought with incredible valour during the first and second land campaigns of the war, taking part to the decisive Battle of Tacna[50]. On 4 January 1880, as a consequence of the brilliant performances of this unit, the government decided to form a 2nd "Atacama" Battalion from the province of Copiapó. On 16 August 1880, however, this new unit was disbanded and absorbed into the original 1st "Atacama" Battalion. With the inclusion of the new soldiers, the latter was transformed into a regiment on 21 August 1880. The new regiment played an important role during the battles of Chorrillos and Miraflores, demonstrating to be one of the best Chilean units and suffering extremely high casualties. Having lost 474 men during the two battles for Lima, the "Atacama" Regiment was finally sent back to Chile, where it was disbanded on 1st April 1881.

National Guard Infantry Battalions "Valdivia" and "Caupolicán": in May 1879 the National Guard Infantry Regiment "Valdivia" was formed as part of the Chilean

Captain of the National Guard Infantry Battalion "Caupolicán".

general mobilization; during September of the same year, however, the regiment was disbanded in order to form two new National Guard battalions. The first, organized on 13 September, was named "Valdivia" as the old regiment; the second, organized on 29 September, was named "Caupolicán". The latter took part to the battles of Chorrillos and Miraflores, before being absorbed into the regular forces as the 9th Infantry Battalion of the Line on 27 October 1881 (with a strength of six companies).

---

50 Greve-Moller P., Fernàndez-Cerda C., *Uniforms of the Pacific War 1879-1884*, Nottingham, 2010

Soldiers of the "Esmeralda" Regiment in skirmishing formation during training.

Lieutenant and sergeant (left) and soldier (above) of the "Esmeralda"; the NCO is wearing the grey greatcoat.

National Guard Infantry Regiment "Esmeralda": initially created on 31 May 1879 in Santiago as "Carampangue" Battalion. On 9 June it was transformed into a regiment (with two battalions) and renamed "Esmeralda" in honour of a Chilean warship that fought valiantly against the Peruvians in the naval battle of Iquique (21 May 1879). The name "Carampangue" was later adopted by a new National Guard Infantry Battalion, which took part to the fourth war campaign. Apparently, the majority of this regiment's young officers came from the elite families of the Chilean capital. During the war campaigns the "Esmeralda" demonstrated to be one of the best National Guard units, taking part with great courage to the battles of Tacna and Chorrillos. After the conquest of Lima, as part of the general reorganization of the Chilean Army and National Guard, the "Esmeralda" Regiment was absorbed into the regular forces as the 7th Infantry Battalion of the Line and reduced to a strength of six companies.

98

Officers and soldiers of the National Guard Infantry Regiment "Chillán".

National Guard Infantry Battalion "Chillán": mobilized between September and October of 1879, this battalion played no active role in the war until taking part to the Battle of Tacna. On 15 August 1880, as a result of the good performances showed on the field of battle, the unit was expanded and transformed into a regiment with two battalions. After fighting in the great battles of Chorrillos and Miraflores, on 22 October 1881 the "Chillán" Regiment was absorbed into the regular forces as the 8th Infantry Battalion of the Line and reduced to a strength of six companies.

National Guard Infantry Battalion "Coquimbo": raised on 30 June 1879 in Coquimbo (with four companies of 150 men each), this battalion included many ex-miners and took part to the first two war

campaigns (including the Battle of Tacna). On 31 August 1880, during the reorganization of the Chilean military forces for the Lima campaign, the "Coquimbo" was transformed into a regiment having two battalions (1st "Coquimbo" and 2nd "Coquimbo"). After participating with great valour to the battles for Lima, the regiment was sent back to Chile and then disbanded. Very soon, however, the Chilean authorities decided to form a new 3rd "Coquimbo" Battalion that was sent to Peru as part of the military forces taking part to the fourth war campaign.

Lieutenant of the National Guard Infantry Regiment "Melipilla".

National Guard Infantry Battalion "Melipilla": mobilized on 7 November 1879, with six companies of 100 men each. Differently from the majority of the other National Guard battalions, it was not transformed into a regiment. The unit took part to the third war campaign, fighting with great valour and suffering very heavy casualties during the battles of Chorrillos and Miraflores. After the battles for Lima (in March 1881) the valorous battalion returned to Chile with several other National Guard units, where it was finally disbanded.

Sergeant of the National Guard Infantry Regiment "Aconcagua".

National Guard Infantry Battalion "Colchagua": created on 14 November 1879 mostly with peasants and farmers, it played no active part in the conflict until being expanded and transformed into a regiment on 14 August 1880 in view of the Lima campaign. Now the unit had two battalions of four companies each. After taking part to the battles of Chorrillos and Miraflores, where it suffered serious losses, the regiment was sent back to Chile and finally disbanded on 1st April 1881.

National Guard Infantry Battalion "Aconcagua": formed on 22 November 1879 with a total of 600 men (mostly peasants and farmers), distributed in six companies of 100 soldiers each. On 26 December 1879 a 2nd "Aconcagua" Battalion was formed with new volunteers coming from the same province, which had the same number of soldiers and structure of the previous unit. Later the two battalions were assembled together in order to form a single "Aconcagua" Regiment. This new unit continued to serve in Peru also after being transformed into a battalion, returning to Chile in 1884.

National Guard Infantry Battalion "Concepción": mobilized on 2 January 1880, with six companies of 100 men each. On 14 October 1880 it was expanded and transformed into a regiment, having two battalions of four companies each. The new unit took part to the third war campaign, fighting with great courage and suffering very heavy losses during the battles of Chorrillos and Miraflores. After the battles for Lima, on 28 March 1881, the unit was again reduced to the strength of a battalion (with 900 men in six companies). It remained to serve in Peru as part of the Chilean occupation forces, taking part to several combat actions against the Peruvian resistance forces (including the decisive Battle of Huamachuco). The valorous battalion returned to Chile in August 1884, where it was finally disbanded.

Sub-lieutenant of the National Guard Infantry Regiment "Concepción".

National Guard Infantry Battalion "Talca": raised on 6 March 1880, with six companies of 100 men each. This unit was mainly composed by farmers and "huasos" (the Chilean term for "gauchos") coming from the countryside of Talca[51]. On 31 August 1880 it was expanded and transformed into a regiment, having two battalions of four companies each. The new unit took part to the third war campaign, fighting with great courage and suffering very heavy losses during the battles of Chorrillos and Miraflores. After the battles for Lima the unit was again reduced to the strength of a battalion due to the heavy losses, but it remained to serve in Peru as part of the Chilean occupation forces. The "Talca" Battalion took part to the last battle of the War of the Pacific, fought at Huamachuco, before being sent back to Chile and disbanded in May 1884.

---

51 Greve-Moller P., Fernàndez-Cerda C., *Uniformes de la Guerra del Pacifico 1879-1884*, Santiago, Chile, 2008

Lieutenant (left) and Captain with campaign equipment (right) of the National Guard Infantry Regiment "Talca".

Captain of the "Talca" Regiment with a captured Peabody-Martini rifle.

Captain of the National Guard Infantry Battalion "Rengo".

National Guard Infantry Battalion "Rengo": mobilized on 6 March 1880, with 600 men in six companies. On 4 September 1880 the unit was expanded and transformed into a regiment, with two battalions of four companies each (named 1st "Rengo" and 2nd "Rengo"). On 29 September, just a few days after its creation, the regiment was disbanded, and the two battalions were ordered to act as independent units. Differently from the majority of the other National Guard battalions, these two units were not present at the great battles of Chorrillos and Miraflores. After the occupation of Lima, on 12 April 1881, the 1st "Rengo" Battalion was disbanded. On 16 August the remaining 2nd Battalion, by now simply known as "Rengo", was augmented with the addition of two companies. It served in Peru as part of the Chilean occupation forces, until returning to Chile in May 1884.

National Guard Infantry Battalion "Curicó": mobilized in March 1880. It numbered 900 men organized into six companies, being one of the largest National Guard battalions of the Chilean Army. After taking part to the battles for Lima (with a marginal role), the unit remained in Peru as part of the Chilean occupation forces. It returned to Chile in June 1884, where it was finally disbanded.

National Guard Infantry Battalion "Victoria": mobilized on 2 August 1880, with six companies of 100 men each. Differently from the majority of the other National Guard battalions, it was not transformed into a regiment. The unit took part to the third war campaign, fighting with great valour and suffering very heavy casualties during the battles of Chorrillos and Miraflores[52]. After the battles for Lima, the valorous battalion remained to serve in Peru as part of the Chilean occupation forces, taking part to several combat actions against the Peruvian resistance forces (including the decisive Battle of Huamachuco). It returned to Chile in June 1884, where it was finally disbanded.

52 Estado Mayor General del Ejercito, *Historia del Ejercito de Chile*, Santiago, Chile, 1980-1983

Officers and flag of the National Guard Infantry Battalion "Victoria".

Sergeant of the National Guard Infantry Battalion "Quillota".

104

National Guard Infantry Battalion "Quillota": mobilized on 2 September 1880, with six companies of 100 men each. Differently from the majority of the other National Guard battalions, it was not transformed into a regiment. The unit took part to the third war campaign, fighting with great valour and suffering very heavy casualties during the battles of Chorrillos and Miraflores. After the battles for Lima (in March 1881) the valorous battalion returned to Chile with several other National Guard units, where it was finally disbanded.

National Guard Infantry Battalion "San Fernando": mobilized on 5 October 1880, with six companies of 150 men each. Unlike the majority of the other National Guard battalions, it was not present at the great battles of Chorrillos and Miraflores. After the occupation of Lima, the unit served in Peru as part of the Chilean occupation forces. It returned to Chile in July 1884, where it was finally disbanded.

National Guard Infantry Battalion "Lontué": mobilized on 6 October 1880, with six companies of 150 men each. Differently from the majority of the other National Guard battalions, it was not present at the great battles of

Sub-lieutenant of the National Guard Infantry Battalion "Lontué" in service dress.

Chorrillos and Miraflores. After the occupation of Lima, the unit served in Peru as part of the Chilean occupation forces. It returned to Chile in June 1884, where it was finally disbanded.

Officers of the National Guard Infantry Battalion "Lontué".

National Guard Infantry Battalion "Maule": organized on 7 October 1880 in Santiago as a regiment, with two battalions of four companies each. Apparently, the members of this unit were mostly ex-tradesmen from the Chilean capital. Unlike the majority of the other National Guard battalions, it was not present at the great battles of Chorrillos and Miraflores. After the occupation of Lima, the unit was reduced to the strength of a battalion and served in Peru as part of the Chilean occupation forces. It returned to Chile in August 1884, where it was finally disbanded.

National Guard Infantry Battalion "Ángeles": mobilized on 9 October 1880, with six companies of 150 men each. Differently from the majority of the other National Guard battalions, it was not transformed into a regiment. The unit took part to the third war campaign, fighting with great valour and suffering very heavy casualties during the battles of Chorrillos and Miraflores. After the battles for Lima, the valorous battalion remained to serve in Peru as part of the Chilean occupation forces. It returned to Chile in August 1884, where it was finally disbanded. Finally, the Chilean National Guard also deployed some mobilized units of cavalry and artillery:

National Guard Cavalry Squadron "Carabineros de Maipú": sent to the front on 30 March 1880, this unit inherited the flag and traditions of the old "Carabineros de la Frontera".

Chilean sergeant in summer campaign dress, with buff desert boots and white trousers.

National Guard Cavalry Squadron "General Las Heras": took part to the fourth war campaign.

National Guard Cavalry Squadron "General Cruz": took part to the fourth war campaign.

National Guard Artillery Brigade "Mejillones": formed in the port of Mejillones after the occupation of Antofagasta, together with the "Antofagasta", "Caracoles" and "Salinas" Battalions. It acted as a garrison unit to protect the newly-conquered coast of the Antofagasta region during the first war campaign, playing no active part in the military operations.

Chilean officers of the 1st Line Infantry Regiment "Buín".

THE CHILEAN ARMY IN THE SECOND PART OF THE WAR

As we have seen, with the outbreak of the hostilities the five, line infantry battalions were transformed into regiments having two battalions of four companies each. Formally two of the latter were of fusiliers, while the other two were of grenadiers and "cazadores" (chasseurs); this traditional subdivision, however, did not exist in practice and all the companies had the same characteristics. Each battalion was to number 600 men and thus each regiment had 1,200 soldiers. Regarding the National Guard, the majority of the early infantry units were all battalions; these could have an organization with four companies (like the line battalions) or a bigger one with six companies (four of fusiliers, one of grenadiers and one of "cazadores"). Before the third war campaign, as part of the general reorganization that saw a further expansion of the Chilean Army in view of the advance on Lima, most of the original National Guard battalions were transformed into regiments having the same internal structure of the regular ones. After the occupation of the Peruvian capital, the units of the National Guard underwent a radical process of reorganization: several were sent back to Chile and disbanded, while others were reduced to the strength of a battalion and continued to serve in Peru. Some of the best National Guard regiments, instead, were included into the regular infantry as line battalions[53]. The original line infantry regiments were again reduced to battalions (including the "Zapadores de

Sergeant of the 1st Line Infantry Regiment "Buín".

53 Greve-Moller P., Fernàndez-Cerda C., *Uniforms of the Pacific War 1879-1884*, Nottingham, 2010

Sergeant of the 1st Line Infantry Regiment "Buín"; the kepi is a National Guard one.

la Frontera" and the Naval Artillery Battalion), with six companies each (four of fusiliers, one of grenadiers and one of "cazadores"); the new line battalions formed from National Guard units received this same new structure (being reduced from regiments to battalions). In addition, all the line battalions of the regular army received a denomination (until that time only the 1st Line Infantry Battalion had a name). This was the new order of battle of the Chilean line infantry resulting from all the changes described above:

- 1st Line Infantry Battalion "Buín"

- 2nd Line Infantry Battalion "Tacna"

- 3rd Line Infantry Battalion "Pisagua"

- 4th Line Infantry Battalion "Arica"

- 5th Line Infantry Battalion "Santiago"

- 6th Line Infantry Battalion "Chacabuco"
(ex-National Guard)

- 7th Line Infantry Battalion "Esmeralda"
(ex-National Guard)

- 8th Line Infantry Battalion "Chillán" (ex-National Guard)

- 9th Line Infantry Battalion "Caupolicán" (ex-National Guard)

- Line Infantry Battalion "Zapadores de la Frontera"

- Naval Artillery Battalion

Chilean officers of the 2nd Line Infantry Regiment.

The other regular units did not change their organization from the beginning until the end of the war: the three cavalry regiments continued to have two squadrons each, including the "Carabineros de Yungay" that had to reform its 1st Squadron after this was captured by the Peruvians. The 1st Artillery Regiment continued to have eight companies (one of which was of mounted artillery), while the 2nd that originally had just five companies (one of which was of garrison artillery) later adopted the same internal structure with eight companies of the 1st Regiment.

*Soldiers of the 2nd Line Infantry Regiment,
with "guerrera" and white-covered kepi.*

*Chilean sub-lieutenant of the
3rd Line Infantry Regiment
in campaign dress.*

*Chilean officers of the 2nd Line
Infantry Regiment in service dress.*

*Chilean soldiers of the 3rd Line
Infantry Regiment in service dress.*

Chilean officers of the 4th Line Infantry Regiment.

Chilean lieutenant-colonel of the 4th Line Infantry Regiment.

Officer of the 4th Line Infantry Regiment with the traditional Chilean "corvo" (knife).

Chilean officers of the 5th Line Infantry Regiment "Santiago".

FORMATION AND COMPOSITION

In general terms, the Chilean Army has one of the most glorious combat histories among the various military forces of South America. It played a very important role in the campaigns for liberation from Spain and showed its efficiency during the second part of the conflict against the Peru-Bolivian Confederation. But, what made the military of Chile an example to follow for all the armies of Latin America were its brilliant victories during the War of the Pacific, the majority of which were obtained against all odds. As we have already seen, the armies of Peru and Bolivia were strongly politicized, and their most recent combat experiences came from the internal conflicts that constantly ravaged their countries. They had a clear numerical superiority over the Chileans, but this was compensated by a series of other important factors. The first and probably most significant one was that the Chilean soldiers had much more combat experience than their Peruvian or Bolivian equivalents. After the end of the war between Chile and the Confederation of Peru-Bolivia, the armies of the two allied countries remained mostly inactive until 1879. If we exclude the 1841 war between them (a direct consequence of the break-up of the Confederation) and a small border war between Peru and Ecuador during 1858-1860, the military forces of Bolivia and Peru were only involved in military coups and internal revolutions[54]. During all this extended period, instead, the Chileans faced an external enemy on a regular basis that was a real threat to the security of their country. The entire southern part of Chile, in fact, was still in the hands of the local Indians: this large region, the equivalent of the Argentine Patagonia, is known as Araucania and had always been inhabited by the most skilled and ferocious native warriors of South America. The various Araucanian tribes, in fact, had been able to repel the Spanish expeditions of conquest for decades and remained independent also after the independence of Chile. They were very rarely collaborative with the Chilean authorities and kept a continuous state of open war on their border with the areas under control of the government. Under all aspects, Chile had an additional southern border with a foreign country, along which most of its military forces were usually garrisoned. The Araucanian Indians, probably the best native light cavalry in the world, launched large and violent raiding expeditions against the Chilean settlements located near the frontier: these caused very serious human and material losses, which tended to stop (at least for a certain period) the push of the Chilean colonists towards south. Despite being little known outside South America, this "Wild West of the Southern Cone" had a very important role in the development of Argentina and Chile as modern nations. These two countries, in fact, had to fight for years in order to conquer a large part of their national territory from the Indians (Patagonia for Argentina and Araucania for Chile); this need strongly affected the developments of those countries' armies, as well as their political life. Being stationed on the Araucanian frontier for all the period 1839-1879, the Chilean military units were gradually able to defeat the Indians and complete the process known as "pacification": despite this name, however, it had very little of pacific since it consisted in a terrible guerrilla war fought with harsh methods. By 1879 the conflict with the Indians was still far from being resolved, but the frontier was under control and the incursions of the natives were not as devastating as before. During these long years of service against the Araucanians the Chilean officers and soldiers gradually learned the same tactics used by their enemies, which were based on mobility and speed. Once sent on the frontier, a young recruit became very soon a reliable veteran: this was particularly true for the cavalry, which played a great part of the fight against the natives. Their quality, built up during many years of combat experience, was not even comparable to that of the Peruvian and Bolivian mounted forces. Training, equipment, weapons and horses of the Chilean cavalry were extremely good: as the War of the Pacific would show, the Chilean veterans of the Araucanian Frontier were to be no match for any opponent.

---

54 Sater, William F., *Andean Tragedy: Fighting the War of the Pacific 1879–1884*, University of Nebraska, 2007

Photo showing Chilean soldiers on the field, during a pause in the combat operations.

Obviously, what we have said above is valid for the regulars only, since the role played by the National Guard in defending the frontier with the Indians was generally quite marginal. As we have already said, the Civic Guard had been created as a balance against the political ambitions of the military leaders. Thanks to it, Chile remained the only country of South America (together with Brazil) that experimented a limited number of internal wars and practically no long period of dictatorial rule. High ranking officers of the army were generally kept outside political life and the spheres of government and military were always separated. The country was under control of its civilian and democratic governments, which could generally rely on the loyalty and support of both the regular army and National Guard. However, we should not forget that the Chilean Army, despite being non-politicized and quite efficient, was always kept on very small numbers by the various governments. This helped to maintain internal stability for several decades but resulted in a serious handicap in case of wars against foreign countries. This was the case of the conflict against the Peru-Bolivian Confederation, but especially of the War of the Pacific. The Chilean regulars were perfectly dressed and equipped, had excellent weapons and training, could rely on a solid combat experience: but they were extremely few. The government's response to this problem was a real miracle, because in a few months the Chileans were able to revitalize the National Guard in an extraordinary way. This was almost cancelled during the serious economic crisis preceding the war but retained a solid structure that was distributed across the whole national territory[55]. Each area of the country had a local command of the Civic Guard, which was known as "Comandancia General de Armas"; on a command level, the National Guard as a whole was under control of the army thanks to a special national commission named "General Inspection of the National Guard". Control of the regulars kept the standards of the Civic Guard at an acceptable level, but this was not so oppressive, and the National Guard units retained a large degree of autonomy. Under all conditions, the Chilean Civic Guard was not comparable to the similar organizations deployed by Peru and Bolivia (which National Guard units were generally quite scarce regarding quality).

55 Lòpez-Urrutia, Carlos, *La Guerra del Pacifico 1879-1884*, Madrid, 2003

To use the existing National Guard structure to its full potential, the Chilean authorities only needed a flow of volunteers wishing to enlist and to serve: this is exactly what happened, since thousands and thousands of Chilean men hurried to the recruiting points with the ambition to serve their country. Patriotism was incredibly strong in Chile, probably more than in any other country of South America: it became even more impressive as soon as the hostilities began, since the war against Peru and Bolivia was generally perceived by the population as a defensive war against a great foreign menace. Chileans had always had a phobia regarding the possible unification of Peru and Bolivia against them; in addition, they had a strong will to help the thousands of expatriated miners who lived and worked as foreigners in the Desert of Atacama (in provinces under Bolivian or Peruvian control). A total of 15,000 Chileans living in Peru and Bolivia were expulsed from those countries at the outbreak of the war: after having all their possessions confiscated by the enemy governments, these Chileans had no alternative but to go back to their home country and enlist in the National Guard (seeking vengeance against the states that had expelled them). According to Chilean law, National Guard units could be employed outside the country only if formally mobilized by Presidential Decree. This limitation, however, was not a problem for the expansion of the National Guard: a large number of Presidential Decrees was promulgated, which enabled the mobilization of many units.

Contemporary drawing showing the entrance of the Chilean cavalry in Lima.

Bearing in mind these general conditions, it is easy to understand how the Chilean authorities were able to form such an impressive number of National Guard infantry units. In addition, we should not forget that most of the manpower used to expand the regular forces at the beginning of the war came from the National Guard: for example, it was thanks to the recruits coming from the Civic Guard that the regular infantry battalions were transformed into regiments. Obviously, the starting level of these volunteers was not comparable to that of the regulars: most of them did not have any military experience or had received just a very superficial training. In any case, their instruction did not start from zero and they soon showed great ability to adapt. In a few months some National Guard units became elite ones, superior in quality and performances to most of the Peruvian or Bolivian regulars. This phenomenon surprised the Chilean high command, which decided to include some of the best National Guard units in the regular forces. Thanks to this incredible mix of veteran regulars and willing National Guardsmen, the War of the Pacific was mostly a series of brilliant Chilean victories (culminating with the occupation of Lima). The last phase of the war, the Sierra Campaign, was the less brilliant for Chilean arms: it was conducted mostly by the regulars, who had serious difficulties in confronting with the skilled Peruvian resistance forces. The Chileans had experience with guerrilla warfare against the Indians, but the environment of the Andes was totally different. Lacking proper knowledge of the

Colonel Alejandro Gorostiaga, Chilean divisional commander at Huamachuco.

terrain and being hated by the local populations, the Chilean soldiers suffered from the peculiar living conditions of the Andes. Despite all these difficulties and after many small defeats, they were eventually able to end the war with a brilliant victory at Huamachuco. After all they had served their country better than in any optimistic assessment. All the above can be referred to the "Mobilized" National Guard, which served together with the regular army and had its same training and weapons. It should not be forgotten, however, that also the "Static" National Guard was fully mobilized and played a very important role during the War of the Pacific. With the regular army entirely deployed in the north against Peru and Bolivia, the Indian frontier with the Araucanian tribes was to remain completely undefended. The Indians, well aware of this new strategic situation, were ready to launch new raids against the Chilean colonists and the latter's' destiny seemed very negative: but the government had no intention of losing the territorial conquests of the previous decades and thus relied heavily on the "Static" Civic Guard to garrison the frontier areas. Despite being poorly equipped and armed, this National Guardsmen were able to keep security and order on the border and inside the other provinces of Chile. The home front is very important in any kind of military conflict and this was particularly true for South American countries: in fact, internal revolutions could easily cause the collapse of the military forces fighting on the front. Thanks to the obscure soldiers of the

"Static" National Guard, Chile was able to avoid all this and to contain the raids of the Indians across the southern border[56]. The home front remained stable and solid, contributing in a decisive way to the positive conclusion of the war effort.

The Chilean Military Academy had been formed as early as 1817 by the father of the Chilean independence, the "libertador" Bernardo O'Higgins. Closed for economic problems in 1819, it opened again in 1831. During the following seven years, it formed a good number of excellent young officers, who showed all their competence and valour during the war against the Peru-Bolivian Confederation. In 1838, fearing to have too many officers (a real political problem for countries like Peru and Bolivia), the Chilean government decided to close again the Academy because the army already had the needed number of officers. In 1842, however, it started to function again and this time on a regular basis that was not affected by any further interruption. The "products" of this new golden age were the competent officers who led the Chilean Army during the Chincha Islands War against Spain and in the War of the Pacific. Since its formation, the Chilean Military Academy was strongly influenced by the French doctrines of the time and generally adopted French traditions and practices. This influence was part of the general French influx, which was apparent in several other aspects (like dress regulations). On 2 November 1876, due to the economic crisis of that year and to a cadet riot, the Academy was closed again but only for a very short period. In 1878, due to the great changes in the international political situation, the government decided to open again the Academy: this continued to work at full speed for the entire duration of the war, training a large number of young officers. Chilean commanders imposed a strict discipline over their men, who were punished with incredible severity in case of desertion or insubordination. As opposed to Peru and Bolivia, Chile did not have a conscription law and all its regular soldiers (both rankers and NCOs) were volunteers who had enlisted in return for a bonus that was provided by the government. In general terms, the Chilean common soldier had a great resilience and could continue under any kind of hardship. Many of the volunteers who enlisted in the "Mobilized" National Guard units were hard workers, like miners or farmers (the "huasos") who had all the capabilities and right potential to become exceptional soldiers. Under the competent guide of their officers, unlike from their Peruvian and Bolivian equivalents, the Chilean volunteers were soon able to become reliable and expert fighting men.

WEAPONS

One of the reasons behind the Chilean victory in the War of the Pacific was with no doubts the absolute superiority in the field of weaponry[57]. Different from Peru and Bolivia, Chile was one of the few South American countries (together with Brazil) that had already standardized the weapons of its regular military forces. This meant that the Chileans did not have any problem deriving from confusion of calibres, which was a real pain in the neck for the poor supply systems of the Allied armies. In 1872 the Chilean government decided to launch a massive program of weapon purchases from Europe, with the clear objective of modernizing the weaponry of its armed forces. In that same year a special military commission was sent to Europe, where it evaluated and compared the various purchase options that were available. The decisions taken by this commission were very intelligent, since they resulted in the purchase and adoption of high quality weapons for the Chilean Army. Between 1873 and 1874 the Chileans completed this massive series of important investments, which were to transform the Chilean Army into the military force of Latin America having the most modern and efficient weapons of all. The standard rifle of the line infantry was the excellent Comblain II manufactured in Belgium; this, however, had been bought only in the number needed to equip the regular line infantry and thus there were no additional ones to arm the National Guard. This, in

---

56 Estado Mayor General del Ejercito, *Historia del Ejercito de Chile*, Santiago, Chile, 1980-1983
57 Sater, William F., *Andean Tragedy: Fighting the War of the Pacific 1879–1884*, University of Nebraska, 2007

fact, was one of the greatest problems faced by the Chileans during the War of the Pacific: as we have seen, the new units of the "Mobilized" National Guard were composed by thousands of men, who needed to be armed with modern rifles before being sent to the war front in the north. The Chilean authorities tried to obtain additional weapons from the Comblain factory, but the latter had too many commissions that slowed down the production. In fact, the Chileans received only 5,180 additional Comblain rifles during the war, which were generally given only to the regular infantry units. As a result of this situation, the Chileans had to search for other supply sources in order to rapidly arm the units of the National Guard. Two European factories were contacted: the Austrian Steyr and the Dutch Beaumont. The first produced the M1874 Gras rifle (standard weapon of the French Army) and the second produced the M1871 Beaumont rifle (standard weapon of the Dutch Army). In total, these two manufacturers produced 21,799 Gras and 9.964 Beaumont rifles: all these weapons were given to the National Guard units, which were thus able to employ high quality weapons exactly as the regulars. The M1874 Gras was nothing else than a modified and improved version of the Chassepot; those produced by Steyr for Chile were all modified in order to use the same ammunitions of the Comblain II rifles. The M1871 Beaumont already had the same calibre of the Comblain II, this being one of the reasons why it was chosen. If the regular army and "Mobilized" National Guard were armed with modern and excellent rifles, the same could not be said of the "Static" National Guard: having to face an enemy like the Araucanian Indians, who had very few modern firearms, the National Guardsmen remaining of garrison in Chile were given the old weapons discarded by the regular forces since 1874. These consisted of old French flintlocks converted into percussion weapons, Minié muskets and British M1866 Snider-Enfield rifles (the breech-loading conversion of the Pattern 1853 Enfield). Apparently, a certain number of Beaumonts was given also to the National Guard units serving on the Indian Frontier, but this happened only later in the war. After the campaign of Lima, most of the National Guard units armed with Gras or Beaumont rifles went back to Chile, while the few remaining to serve with the regulars in Peru were generally re-equipped with Comblains. As a result, almost all the Chilean soldiers fighting in the fourth war campaign carried a Comblain II rifle.

The mechanism of the excellent Belgian Comblain II rifle, employed by Chile.

The "special" units of the Chilean infantry had some peculiarities in their equipment: the "Zapadores de la Frontera", for example, were armed with Comblain II rifles but had a peculiar saw bayonet. This had a serrated blade that could be used to cut wood or straw and for cutting dense undergrowth[58]. The soldiers of the Naval Artillery were individually equipped with Comblains, but also manned a certain number of bronze guns independently from the army's artillery. The Chilean cavalry was equipped with two different models of carbines: the "Granaderos a Caballo" had M1866 Winchesters, while the "Cazadores a Caballo" used M1860 Spencers. The new "Carabineros de Yungay" Regiment received M1866 Winchesters. As the war progressed, the old Winchesters employed by the cavalry were replaced by new ones of the 1873 model that were gradually bought (for a total of 4,868). The standard cavalry sabre was the French M1839 Chatellerault, 1,000 of which had been bought in Europe by the mission sent in 1872. Apparently the new "Carabineros de Yungay" were initially supplied with old British M1796 light cavalry sabers; later in the war they received the same Chatellerault ones of the other cavalry units. Chilean officers of any unit received no standard weapons from the government and thus were armed with privately-purchased swords and Colt, Lefaucheux or Galand revolvers.

A Chilean battery of the 2nd Artillery Regiment, with Krupp M1879 field guns of 75mm.

---

58 Greve-Moller P., Fernàndez-Cerda C., *Uniforms of the Pacific War 1879-1884*, Nottingham, 2010

118

Two Gatling machine guns manned by Chilean gunners of the 2nd Artillery Regiment.

The purchasing mission sent to Europe in 1872 had decided to adopt the excellent Krupp guns as new artillery system of the Chilean Army. By 1879 the Chileans could deploy the following Krupp guns: twelve M1873 mountain guns of 60mm, twelve M1873 field guns of 87mm and four M1867 field guns of 78.5mm. In addition, the Chilean artillery could count on several La Hitte rifled guns that had been purchased in 1868: eight M1858 mountain guns of 86.5mm and four M1858 field guns of 84mm. As a reserve, there were also twelve bronze guns of 87mm (apparently local copies of the M1858 La Hitte mountain guns). With the outbreak of the war, the Chileans faced an increasing need for new artillery pieces (especially to equip the new 2nd Artillery Regiment). As a result, intensive purchases continued also during the first years of the conflict: six Krupp M1879 mountain guns of 75mm, thirty-two Krupp M1880 mountain guns of 75mm, eight Krupp M1879 field guns of 75mm, twenty-one Krupp M1880 field guns of 75mm, twenty-four Krupp M1880 field guns of 87mm and six Armstrong M1880 mountain guns of 66mm. Thanks to the massive use of the Krupp artillery system, the Chileans had no rivals in South America regarding superiority in this particular field. In addition to the above, the Chilean artillery could also deploy six Gatling and two Nordenfeldt machine guns. Single artillerymen were armed with the same M1866 Winchester carbines of the cavalry, which were later replaced by new M1873 ones. It is interesting to note that at the beginning of the war the Chilean artillerymen had several difficulties in using the new Krupp guns and Gatling machine guns in a proper way: these new weapons, after being bought, had been stored in magazines without seeing any use for training. As a result, the Chilean artillerymen had to learn how to employ them on the field of battle, adapting themselves to the new tactics deriving from their use.

UNIFORMS

Since the dress regulations of 1817, promulgated by Bernardo O'Higgins and completed in 1819, the uniforms of the newly-independent Chilean Army had been heavily influenced by contemporary French models and fashions. This tendency was confirmed by the dress regulations of 1823, which prescribed simple but elegant uniforms and confirmed dark blue as the dominant colour of Chilean military dress. With the exception of some modifications introduced for mounted units in 1827 and 1832, the uniforms prescribed in 1823 were retained until 1852 (thus being worn also during the conflict against the Peru-Bolivian Confederation). In 1852 new dress regulations were promulgated, which were a real revolution for the uniforms of the Chilean Army[59]. These were inspired by the French ones of 1845, which were admired and copied by several South American states. Chile was one of the first countries that took part to this process, modernizing its military dress and adopting a very French-looking appearance. The 1852 regulations were completed in 1858, when the red kepi was formally introduced together with the use of different colours to distinguish branches of service. The uniforms prescribed in 1852 were extremely modern for their time and thus remained in use until being substituted in 1878, shortly before the outbreak of the War of the Pacific. Apparently, however, cavalry units continued to wear the 1852 uniforms as parade dress also after the adoption of the new ones in 1878 (we have evidence of cavalry soldiers wearing 1852 dress on parade as late as the end of the War of the Pacific). The 1852 regulations prescribed the following uniform for the infantry: black shako with brass unit number on the front, national cockade, yellow lace holder, red top band, brass chinscales and pompom in company colour (yellow for fusiliers, red for grenadiers and green for "cazadores"). The shako of officers was slightly different, since it had golden rings showing rank and additional laurel branches around the golden unit number. Dark blue single-breasted frock-coat with red frontal piping, collar and round cuffs, having brass buttons and unit number on the collar. The unit number was reproduced also on the brass buckle of the black leather waist belt. "Garance" red trousers (in perfect French style) and black shoes. During summer, as usual, white trousers were usually worn. Rank was shown by golden inverted "chevrons" (piped in red) on the cuffs. Officers, instead, wore golden epaulettes and contre-epaulettes with white fringes as rank distinctions.

The cavalry uniforms were quite different but extremely elegant: black shako with brass unit badge on the front (a "chasseur" horn for the "Cazadores a Caballo" and a flaming grenade for the "Granaderos a Caballo"), national cockade, yellow lace holder, top band in green or red (according to the regiment), brass chinscales and pompom in green or red (according to the regiment). The shakos of officers had golden rank rings. Dark blue double-breasted coatee with detachable frontal plastron and short turnbacks, having brass buttons and dark blue round cuffs. Frontal plastron, collar, cuff flaps, piping to cuffs and turnbacks were all in red for Mounted Grenadiers and in green for Mounted Chasseurs. Trousers were "garance" red, with green piping for "Cazadores" and dark blue one for "Granaderos". Soldiers and NCOs had epaulettes in green or red, while officers had golden epaulettes and contre-epaulettes showing their rank. All the belts of the cavalry were white, while boots were in black leather. The short-lived "Lanceros de Colchagua" wore a very peculiar and ornate uniform, copied from that worn by the contemporary French lancers: black "czapska" with brass frontal plate (showing an eagle) and chinscales, having red top part piped in yellow and national cockade. A long yellow falling plume and decorative golden cords and flounders completed the headgear. The rest of the uniform was quite similar to that worn by the other cavalry units, albeit with yellow as distinctive colour: dark blue double-breasted coatee with detachable frontal plastron and short

59 Estado Mayor General del Ejercito, *Historia del Ejercito de Chile*, Santiago, Chile, 1980-1983

turnbacks, having brass buttons and dark blue round cuffs. Frontal plastron, collar, cuff flaps, piping to cuffs and turnbacks were all in yellow. Trousers were "garance" red, with yellow piping; black leather boots. Epaulettes were yellow for soldiers and golden for officers. All the belts were white. The pennants of the lances showed the Chilean national flag. Artillery uniforms were of the same cut of the cavalry ones but had pointed cuffs instead of the round ones with cuff flaps worn by mounted units: black shako with brass unit badge on the front (two crossed cannons under a flaming grenade), national cockade, yellow lace holder, red top band and pompom, brass chinscales. The shakos of officers had golden rank rings around them. The artillery badge was repeated on the brass buckle of the waist belt. Dark blue double-breasted coatee with detachable frontal plastron and short turnbacks, having brass buttons and dark blue round cuffs. Frontal plastron was white while the collar, pointed cuffs and turnbacks were all red. Trousers were dark blue, with red piping. Soldiers and NCOs had epaulettes in red, while officers had golden epaulettes and contre-epaulettes showing their rank. All the belts of the artillery were black, as well as boots. The few officers who made up the Engineer Corps wore the same uniform as their artillery colleagues, but with a double brass tower as distinctive unit badge. On parade, officers of all the branches of service frequently substituted the shako with a black bicorn hat, having national cockade, gold embroidery and white ostrich-feather plume (the latter for superior officers only).

The modifications of 1858 introduced some significant albeit minor changes to the uniforms of the Chilean Army. The red kepi was formally adopted as standard headgear for all the branches of service, being prescribed for use on service and on campaign. As a result, the shako continued to be worn only on parade. The kepi was "garance" red for all infantry and cavalry units but had bottom band in distinctive colours: light blue for infantry, dark blue for Mounted Grenadiers and green for Mounted Chasseurs. The artillery, instead, wore an entirely dark blue kepi. On the front of the new headgear each unit had its distinctive badge in brass: unit number for the infantry, flaming grenade for the Mounted Grenadiers, "chasseur" horn for the Mounted Chasseurs and two crossed cannons under a flaming grenade for artillery[60]. The kepi became extremely popular in a very short time, being very comfortable to wear and easier to produce than a shako. Officer showed their rank on it thanks to golden quarter-piping in French style. As an alternative to the uniforms described above, the Chilean officers and soldiers could also wear a simpler dress designed for use on service or on campaign. This consisted of an entirely dark blue double-breasted redingote for officers, having brass buttons and a dark blue frontal plastron similar in shape to the coloured one worn with the parade uniform. The redingote was extremely simple, since it had no epaulettes or contre-epaulettes (rank was shown only by the golden piping on the kepi); in addition, its collar and round cuffs were entirely dark blue. The service/campaign dress of the soldiers, instead, consisted of an entirely dark blue single-breasted jacket having brass buttons, which was worn together with red or white trousers (depending on season). On 18 December 1869 the Chilean officers were authorized to wear a new model of campaign dress, which had already developed as a non-regulation uniform during the long years of war on the Indian Frontier. This new campaign uniform, copied from that worn by officers of the Navy, was extremely simple and comfortable to wear. Its headgear was a simple dark blue wide-brimmed hat, having the unit badge embroidered in black on the front. Entirely dark blue double-breasted frock-coat with black buttons and dark blue step collar. White shirt and black bow tie; rank was shown by simple shoulder bars. As for the uniform comprising the redingote, trousers were of the same kind worn on parade.

60 Greve-Moller P., Fernàndez-Cerda C., *Uniformes de la Guerra del Pacifico 1879-1884*, Santiago, Chile, 2008

THE 1878 DRESS REGULATIONS

Shortly before the outbreak of the War of the Pacific, on 19 October 1878, the Chilean Army introduced new dress regulations. These were modelled on the contemporary French patterns[61], in spite of the fact that the French Army had been decisively defeated by the Prussians just a few years before. In other words, if the French defeat had led the Peruvians to adopt new Prussian uniforms, it had not changed at all the Chilean positive attitude towards French military fashions and traditions (which remained the same until 1898, when the progressive "Prussianization" of the Chilean armed forces officially started). As a result of this situation, the Chilean soldiers who marched to the front in 1879 were dressed very similarly to their French equivalents of 1870. By the beginning of the hostilities all the Chilean military units had already received the new uniforms of the 1878 model: this was something extremely remarkable, especially if we bear in mind that the Chilean Army of the time did not have any kind of administrative or logistical organization. This changed only with the beginning of the war, because on 5 May 1879 the "General Supply Corps of the Army and Navy on campaign" was officially formed. Despite being created very late and having no previous experience, the Chilean Supply Corps performed extremely well since its beginnings, providing all the Chilean soldiers and sailors taking part to the war with the needed amounts of uniforms, equipment, weapons, ammunitions and food. Initially intended as a provisional organization in existence for the duration of the war, due to its great achievements the "Intendencia" was later confirmed as a stable branch of the Chilean military forces. All the pre-war Chilean uniforms of the 1878 model were produced by the famous Godillot firm of Paris, which had a special contract with Chile. This meant top quality and elegance.

Infantry: The parade uniform consisted of a dark blue shako with red quarter-piping, having red pompom and lace holder. National cockade, brass unit number, black leather top band, visor and chinstrap. Dark blue double-breasted tunic with brass buttons and unit number on collar; red piping to collar, round cuffs and front. The unit number was reproduced also on the brass buckle of the black leather waist belt. "Garance" red trousers with dark blue piping, white spats and black leather shoes. Rank was shown by red inverted "chevrons" on the cuffs. After all a quite simple but extremely elegant uniform. The parade uniform of officers comprised a dark blue shako with golden quarter-piping showing rank; golden pompom and lace holder. National cockade, golden unit number, black leather top band, visor and chinstrap. Dark blue double-breasted tunic with golden buttons and unit number on the collar; red piping to collar, round cuffs and front. The buckle of the black leather waist belt was decorated with a star (of the same kind depicted on the Chilean national flag). "Garance" red trousers with dark blue piping, black leather shoes. Rank was shown by golden epaulettes (with white fringes) or contre-epaulettes and by golden rings around the cuffs.

The campaign uniform prescribed by the 1878 regulations, known in Chile as "guerrera", was extremely simple but also very comfortable for use on the field. It was worn also as service dress. Red kepi with dark blue bottom band and piping, bearing a brass unit number on the front and having black leather visor. Dark blue single-breasted short jacket, having brass buttons and red collar. Red piping to front and round cuffs. The unit number was reproduced also on the brass buckle of the black leather waistbelt. "Garance" red trousers with dark blue piping, black leather shoes. On the campaign uniform rank was shown by yellow inverted "chevrons" on the cuffs. The campaign uniform of officers was similar, but obviously more ornate: red kepi with dark blue bottom band and golden quarter-piping (according to rank); golden unit number on the front and chinstrap, black leather visor. Dark blue double-breasted short tunic, having golden buttons. Red collar and round cuffs, no piping to the front. Golden shoulder bars showing rank. "Garance" red trousers with dark blue piping, black leather boots. During summer white trousers were commonly worn.

---

61 Estado Mayor General del Ejercito, *Historia del Ejercito de Chile*, Santiago, Chile, 1980-1983

"Zapadores de la Frontera": the uniform of these combat engineers was a curious mix of elements coming from the dress of both line infantry and artillery. Dark blue kepi with red quarter-piping, brass unit badge on the front (a letter "Z") and black leather visor. Dark blue double-breasted short jacket with brass buttons; red piping to collar and round cuffs. Dark blue trousers with red double side-stripe, black leather shoes. The brass buckle of the black leather waistbelt bore the same unit badge worn on the kepi.

Naval Artillery Battalion: the uniform of the naval artillerymen, introduced on 8 August 1877, was similar in cut and colour to that of the line infantry but had some distinctive features[62]. Dark blue kepi with grey bottom band and brass unit badge on the front (consisting of a crossed cannon-and-anchor under a star and within a circle of laurels). Dark blue double-breasted short jacket with brass buttons; grey collar, pointed cuffs and frontal piping. Yellow decorative piping to cuffs. Dark blue trousers with grey piping, buff leather boots. The brass buckle of the black leather waistbelt bore the same unit badge worn on the kepi. Officers of this unit were dressed as their equivalents of the Chilean Navy (with uniforms copied from the contemporary dress regulations of the Royal Navy). Their uniform was as follows: dark blue peaked cap with golden chinstrap, quarter-piping (according to rank) and naval emblem on the front (the same worn by

Chilean lieutenant of the Naval Artillery Regiment.

soldiers on the kepi). Dark blue double-breasted frock-coat with golden buttons and dark blue step collar. Grey piping to front, round cuffs, bottom edge and step collar. Rank was shown by golden rings around the cuffs and golden shoulder bars. White shirt and black tie. Dark blue trousers with grey piping and black leather shoes.

Cavalry: the parade uniform of mounted units was very smart and modern, being copied from the dress worn by contemporary French light cavalry (according to the 1872 dress regulations). It consisted of a "Garance" red shako with bottom band and piping in the distinctive colour of each unit (dark blue for "Granaderos a Caballo", green for "Cazadores a Caballo" and light blue for "Carabineros de Yungay"). On the front it had national cockade, pompom and lace holder in the distinctive colour of each unit, brass unit badge (a flaming grenade for "Granaderos a Caballo", a "chasseur" horn for "Cazadores a Caballo" and a crossed saber-and-carbine within a circle of laurels for "Carabineros de Yungay"). Dark blue dolman with black frontal frogging and three rows of brass buttons. Frontal and bottom edges in black, collar and pointed cuffs piped in the distinctive colour of each unit. Brass unit badge on the collar. "Garance" red trousers with piping in the unit's distinctive colour. Black leather boots and white belts. Rank was shown by yellow inverted "chevrons" piped in red and worn on the cuffs. The parade uniform of officers was quite similar, but had the following peculiarities: piping, pompom, lace holder, chinstrap and unit badge of the shako were in gold; the dolman was longer than that worn by soldiers and had golden buttons. The unit badge on collar was golden. Rank was shown by golden Hungarian knots on the sleeves and by golden shoulder boards. Additional golden cords and flounders were worn.

---

62 Greve-Moller P., Fernàndez-Cerda C., *Uniforms of the Pacific War 1879-1884*, Nottingham, 2010

The Line Cavalry Regiment "Granaderos a Caballo".

Trooper of the "Granaderos a Caballo" Regiment, wearing "guerrera". Drawing by Benedetto Esposito.

Corporal of the "Cazadores a Caballo" Regiment, with M1852 uniform.

Lieutenant of the "Granaderos a Caballo" Regiment, wearing M1878 parade dress.

125

Sergeants of the "Carabineros de Yungay" (right and left) and ensign of the "Cazadores a Caballo" (centre), respectively in campaign and service dress according to the 1878 dress regulations. The carbine is a captured Remington one.

The "guerrera" (campaign uniform), instead, was extremely simple but perfect for use on the field. It consisted of a "Garance" red kepi with bottom band and quarter-piping in the distinctive colour of each unit; in addition, this had a brass unit badge on the front. Chinstrap and visor were in black leather. Dark blue single-breasted stable jacket with brass buttons; frontal piping, collar and pointed cuffs in the distinctive colour of each unit. Brass unit badge on the collar. "Garance" red trousers with piping in the unit's distinctive colour, black leather boots and white leather belts. Rank was shown by yellow inverted "chevrons" worn on the cuffs (with no red piping). The campaign uniform of officers was quite similar but had the following peculiarities: quarter-piping (according to rank), chinstrap and unit badge of the kepi were all golden; buttons of the jacket were golden as well as the unit badge on collar. Rank was shown by golden rings around the cuffs and by golden shoulder bars.

Ensign of the "Cazadores a Caballo" Regiment wearing service dress. Drawing by Benedetto Esposito.

Corporal of the "Carabineros de Yungay" Regiment wearing service dress.

127

*Chilean artilleryman wearing the
pre-war M1852 parade uniform.*

*Officers from the 1st Artillery Regiment
wearing service or parade uniform.*

Foot Artillery: the 1878 dress regulations prescribed different uniforms for the companies of foot artillery and for that of horse artillery. Those of the foot artillery were very similar to the dress worn by the infantry. Parade uniform: dark blue shako with red quarter-piping, having red pompom and lace holder. National cockade, brass unit badge (two crossed cannons), black leather top band, visor and chinstrap. Dark blue double-breasted tunic with brass buttons and unit badge on collar; red piping to collar, round cuffs and front. The unit badge was reproduced also on the brass buckle of the black leather waistbelt. Dark blue trousers with red double side-stripe, white spats and black leather shoes. The new 2nd Artillery Regiment received this same uniform but with red trousers piped in dark blue. Rank was shown by red inverted "chevrons" on the cuffs. The parade uniform of officers comprised a dark blue shako with golden quarter-piping showing rank; golden pompom and lace holder. National cockade, golden unit badge (a flaming grenade over two crossed cannons), black leather top band, visor and chinstrap. Dark blue double-breasted tunic with golden buttons and unit badge on the collar; red piping to collar, round cuffs and front. The buckle of the black leather waistbelt was decorated with unit badge. Dark blue trousers with red double side-stripe, black leather shoes. Rank was shown by golden epaulettes (with white fringes) or contre-epaulettes and by golden rings around the cuffs.

Chilean colonel from the 1st Artillery Regiment in parade dress.

Officers from the mounted company of the 1st Artillery Regiment in parade dress.

The campaign uniform was as follows: entirely dark blue kepi with red piping, bearing a brass unit badge on the front (two crossed cannons) and having black leather visor. Dark blue single-breasted short jacket, having brass buttons. Red piping to collar and round cuffs. The unit badge was reproduced also on the brass buckle of the black leather waistbelt. Dark blue trousers with red double side-stripe, black leather shoes. The 2nd Artillery Regiment had entirely red trousers. On the campaign uniform rank was shown by yellow inverted "chevrons" on the cuffs. The campaign uniform of officers was similar, but obviously more ornate: entirely dark blue kepi with golden quarter-piping (according to rank); golden unit badge (a flaming grenade over two crossed cannons) on the front and chinstrap, black leather visor. Dark blue double-breasted short tunic, having golden buttons. Red piping to collar and round cuffs, no piping to the front. Golden shoulder bars showing rank. Dark blue trousers with red double side-stripe, black leather boots.

Horse Artillery: the uniforms of horse artillery were very similar to those of cavalry, albeit with some minor differences. Parade dress was as follows[63]: dark blue shako with single red "chevron" on each side, national cockade and black top band. Red pompom and lace holder, black leather visor and chinstrap. Brass

63 Estado Mayor General del Ejercito, *Historia del Ejercito de Chile*, Santiago, Chile, 1980-1983

*Soldier from the 1st Artillery
Regiment with M1878 service dress.*

*Soldier from the 2nd Artillery
Regiment with M1878 service dress.*

130

Officers of the 2nd Artillery Regiment wearing campaign uniforms.

Officers of the 2nd Artillery Regiment wearing campaign dress.

unit badge on the front, consisting of two crossed cannons. Dark blue dolman with black frontal frogging and three rows of brass buttons. Frontal and bottom edges in black, collar and pointed cuffs piped in red. Brass unit badge on the collar. Dark blue trousers with red double side-stripe (red with dark blue piping for 2nd Regiment), black leather boots and black belts. Rank was shown by yellow inverted "chevrons" piped in red and worn on the cuffs. The parade uniform of officers was quite similar, but had the following peculiarities: pompom, lace holder, top band, chinstrap, unit badge (a flaming grenade over two crossed cannons) and single "chevron" of the shako were in gold; in addition, the headgear had golden rank piping around its base. The dolman was longer than that worn by soldiers and had golden buttons. The unit badge on collar was golden. Rank was shown by golden Hungarian knots on the sleeves and by golden shoulder boards. Additional golden cords and flounders were worn.

The "guerrera" (campaign uniform) consisted of an entirely dark blue kepi with red quarter-piping, which had brass unit badge on the front (two crossed cannons). Chinstrap and visor were in black leather. Dark blue single-breasted stable jacket with brass buttons; frontal piping, collar and pointed cuffs in red. Brass unit badge on the collar. Dark blue trousers with red double side-stripe (entirely red for 2nd Regiment), black leather boots and black belts. The unit badge of the kepi was reproduced also on the brass buckle of the waistbelt. Rank was shown by yellow inverted "chevrons" worn on the cuffs (with no red piping). The campaign uniform of officers was quite similar but had the following peculiarities: quarter-piping (according to rank), chinstrap and unit badge of the kepi (a flaming grenade over two crossed cannons) were all golden; buttons of the jacket were golden as well as the unit badge on collar. Rank was shown by golden rings around the cuffs and by golden shoulder bars.

Officers of the General Staff and of the Engineer Corps: different from the Peruvians and Bolivians, the Chileans had an organized General Staff that had its own peculiar uniform. This was as follows: black bicorn hat with golden embroidery and white ostrich-feather plumes. Entirely dark blue double-breasted tunic with golden buttons and unit badge on the collar (representing the Chilean national shield). White sash worn around the waist, having gold tassels and knots. Rank was shown by golden rings around the cuffs and by golden shoulder boards. Dark blue trousers with golden piping and black leather shoes.

The few officers of the Engineer Corps had a very similar uniform: black bicorn hat with golden embroidery and red ostrich-feather plumes. Dark blue double-breasted tunic with black collar and round cuffs. Golden buttons and unit badge on the collar (representing a castle with two towers). The collar had additional golden embroidery. Red sash worn around the waist, having gold tassels and knots. Rank was shown by golden rings around the cuffs and by golden shoulder boards. Dark blue trousers with red double side-stripe and black leather shoes.

WAR MODIFICATIONS

As we have already said, the War of the Pacific was mostly fought in the Desert of Atacama or in the high Andes of central Peru. The weather conditions of these environments tested the uniforms of the confronting armies to the limit, with extremely hot temperatures during the day and sub-zero ones at night. The Allied military forces were never able to supply their men with appropriate clothing and equipment, while the Chileans did of their best in this sense since the beginning of the war[64]. The set of personal items prescribed by the 1878 dress regulations already included two "special" elements for use during winter and during summer, which were to be of fundamental importance and were extremely useful during the War of the Pacific. For winter, Chilean foot soldiers could count on a very resistant thick greatcoat with

---

64 Greve-Moller, Patricio, *Equipamiento Chileno en la Guerra del Pacifico 1879-1884*, Santiago, Chile, 2014

a detachable hood. This was perfect to face the cold temperatures of the Peruvian winter and thus saw extensive use during the fourth campaign of the conflict. It was entirely grey and could be single-breasted or double-breasted, having no additional decorations but only brass buttons. When wearing the greatcoat, rank "chevrons" were removed from the uniform and applied on it. Officers had a similar item of dress, but their greatcoat included a mantle closed by four buttons to protect the shoulders. Mounted soldiers replaced the greatcoat with coloured and striped "ponchos". Non-regulation neck kerchiefs and scarves, of every possible form and colour, were universally worn around the neck together with the greatcoat (for protection of the face from cold and sand). For summer, Chilean soldiers (from either foot or mounted units) could use a specifically designed tropical uniform: this was made of linen or drill, being entirely white. It consisted of a short single-breasted jacket with brass buttons and trousers.

After all the Chileans were quite well prepared for campaigning in the rough terrains located north of their national territory; the needs of war, however, soon led to the introduction of new uniform items that became extremely popular. The first modifications dictated by practice regarded the headgear: the red kepis, albeit being elegant and fashionable, were not practical for use on campaign. As a result, since the occupation of Antofagasta, Chilean soldiers started to use white covers generally having a curtain for protection of the neck. Usually these had unit number/badge written in black on the front, but entirely white ones were also in use. Sometimes soldiers preferred to continue wearing their old kepis without covers but attached the white drape on the back of them for protection of the neck. Officers, instead, generally replaced their kepis with white tropical pith helmets made of cork. One of the other major changes affected footwear: the black leather shoes of foot units and knee-high boots of mounted troops proved to be completely inadequate for use in the Atacama Desert; as a result, these were replaced by new half-boots made of buff. The latter soon became very popular and were worn by every Chilean soldier deployed on the front.

The Chilean government did not promulgate any new dress regulations during the conflict, but soon after the end of the first war campaign it became clear to all the observers that the old dark blue uniforms with red trousers were not practical for use in the Atacama Desert. As a result, between the second and third war campaign in 1880, all the Chilean units were issued with a new campaign uniform specifically created for use on the northern theatre of operations[65]. This new dress was comfortable, hygienic and cheap to produce, being made with very resistant light blue-grey cloth imported in large quantities from France. It soon became standard issue during the Lima campaign and was universally worn during the fourth war campaign. The new 1880 campaign uniform for the infantry was as follows: entirely light blue-grey kepi with brass unit number/badge on the front; light blue-grey double-breasted tunic with red collar and round cuffs, having brass buttons; entirely light blue-grey trousers and buff leather boots. The front of the tunic could be piped in red, but generally it was not. A brass unit number/badge was frequently worn on the collar. Rank was shown as on the previous campaign uniforms. Apparently, a certain number of these new uniforms were produced with brown cloth during the Lima campaign, due to the shortage of the new light blue-grey cloth imported from France. The version of the 1880 campaign dress worn by mounted units was very similar to that described above: entirely light blue-grey kepi with brass unit badge on the front; light blue-grey short jacket with three rows of brass buttons, having collar and pointed cuffs in the distinctive colour of each unit; entirely light blue-grey trousers with piping in the unit's distinctive colour and buff leather boots. The front of the jacket could be piped in the colour of the unit, but generally it was not.

The adoption of this new uniform was not the only modification introduced by the time of the Lima campaign. The Chilean Army had gradually transformed itself into a very large force, comprising dozens

---

65 Greve-Moller P., Fernàndez-Cerda C., *Uniforms of the Pacific War 1879-1884*, Nottingham, 2010

of different units that had to be organized into divisions. For this reason, to have a clear identification of the various units on the field of battle, new tactical marks were introduced on all Chilean uniforms since 11 January 1881. These were of two different kinds: the divisional ones, indicating the division of the army to which each unit belonged, and the unit ones, which identified each single regiment or battalion. Divisional marks consisted of white horizontal parallel stripes: two for 2nd Division, three for 3rd Division and so on. Unit marks were red (rarely white) and consisted of many different symbols, several of which showed a clear Masonic influence. Divisional devices were worn on the right arm only, while unit ones were generally worn on both arms between the shoulder and the elbow. The "Carabineros de Yungay" was the only unit to wear divisional marks on the cuff. After the conquest of Lima, these tactical marks were not retained.

NATIONAL GUARD UNIFORMS

In general, the various National Guard units used exactly the same kind of uniforms and personal equipment employed by the line units. The Chilean Civic Guard did not have autonomous dress regulations, so its uniforms were copied from those of the regulars with very little modifications. The only noticeable elements that distinguished National Guard units were the colours of their kepis and trousers: while regular units had red kepis with dark blue bottom band and piping, National Guard ones had dark blue kepis with red bottom band and piping. Trousers, instead, were red with dark blue piping for the regulars and dark blue with red piping for the National Guard. Badges were obviously different but ranks and tactical marks were exactly the same employed by the regulars. The universal unit badge of the Civic Guard was the Chilean star, as shown on the national flag: this was reproduced on the front of kepi, buckle of the waistbelt (where it was surrounded by an inscription with the unit's name) and buttons. Sometimes, however, it was replaced by the initials of the unit's name. It is interesting to note that at the beginning of the war some National Guard units tended to have peculiar uniforms, which were quite different from those of the regulars; as the war progressed, especially for the Lima campaign, these more original uniforms were gradually replaced by the standard light blue-grey campaign dress used by the majority of units. In this section we will describe only the uniforms that were different from those of the regulars:

1st National Guard Infantry Battalion "Antofagasta": the uniform of this reserve unit, which never took part to the military operations, was one of the most peculiar in the entire Chilean Army. The headgear consisted of captured Peruvian "Pickelhaube" helmets, five hundred of which had been confiscated by the Chilean authorities: these had been sent from Germany but were blocked in the port of Valparaiso when the war between Chile and Peru started[66]. The captured helmets (which frontal plate was modified to have the Chilean star on the front) were initially given to the National Guard Battalion "Chacabuco", but this soon adopted kepi as new headgear and thus they passed to the "Antofagasta" Battalion. Despite some initial opposition, the "Pickelhaube" was soon loved by the members of this unit; years later, after the Prussianization of the armed forces, all Chilean soldiers would wear this kind of helmet. The rest of the uniform was as follows: light brown (almost khaki) single-breasted jacket with brass buttons; red collar, round cuffs and shoulder straps (this was probably the only Chilean unit to have shoulder straps). Light brown trousers, black leather shoes. The black leather waistbelt had a brass buckle bearing unit number (a "1"). Officers wore a similar but distinct uniform: white pith helmet with golden chinstrap and unit number on the front; double breasted light brown tunic with golden buttons; red collar, round cuffs and shoulder straps; golden unit number on collar and rank stripes on the shoulder straps; light brown trousers, black shoes; black leather waistbelt having buckle decorated with the Chilean star.

---

66 Greve-Moller P., Fernàndez-Cerda C., *Uniformes de la Guerra del Pacifico 1879-1884*, Santiago, Chile, 2008

National Guard Infantry Battalion "Bulnes": kepi having white cover and neck curtain, with a letter "B" written in black on the front. Medium blue single-breasted jacket with brass buttons; dark blue collar and round cuffs. Brass unit badge on the collar (a letter "B"). Medium blue trousers, buff leather boots. The brass buckle of the black leather waistbelt was decorated with a Chilean star encircled by the inscription "GUARDIA MUNICIPAL DE SANTIAGO". The uniform described above was donated to this unit by one of the richest Chilean women of the time, Isidora Goyenechea, who guided a real industrial empire in her country.

National Guard Infantry Battalion "Valparaiso": dark blue kepi with red bottom band, bearing brass unit badge (consisting of the letters "B" and "V" with a Chilean star in the middle). Dark blue single-breasted jacket with brass buttons, having red collar and round cuffs. Dark blue trousers, buff leather boots. The brass buckle of the black leather waistbelt was decorated by a Chilean star encircled by the inscription "GUARDIA MUNICIPAL DE VALPARAISO".

National Guard Infantry Battalion "Chacabuco": when formed in Santiago, this elite unit received a very peculiar uniform that included the Peruvian "Pickelhaube" helmets confiscated in Valparaiso. On 12 July 1879, however, these were replaced by kepis of the usual model worn by National Guard units; as we have seen, the Prussian helmets were given to the "Antofagasta" Battalion that retained them for longer time. The rest of this battalion's uniform was as follows: dark blue single-breasted jacket with brass buttons, having green collar, round cuffs and frontal piping. White trousers with green piping, black shoes. This battalion adopted the standard campaign dress of the regulars in August 1879.

National Guard Infantry Battalion "Navales": the uniform of this veteran National Guard unit was very similar to that of the regular Naval Artillery Battalion, having grey as piping colour. It was as follows: dark blue kepi with grey quarter-piping and brass unit badge on the front (an anchor). Dark blue double-breasted short jacket with brass buttons and grey collar, having grey piping to front and pointed cuffs. Grey trousers with red piping, black shoes. Officers of this unit were dressed as their equivalents of the Chilean Navy (with uniforms copied from the contemporary dress regulations of the Royal Navy). Their uniform was as follows: dark blue peaked cap with golden chinstrap, quarter-piping (according to rank) and unit badge on the front (an anchor surrounded by laurels). Dark blue double-breasted frock-coat with golden buttons and dark blue step collar. Rank was shown by golden rings around the cuffs and golden shoulder bars. White shirt and black tie. Dark blue trousers and black leather shoes.

National Guard Infantry Battalion "Cazadores del Desierto": the uniform of this battalion was extremely peculiar and showed a strong foreign influence. It consisted of a kepi with white cover and neck curtain, having the letters "CdD" written in black on the front. Grey double-breasted short jacket with brass buttons, having green collar and round cuffs. White scarf and trousers, buff leather boots. The outfit of officers was quite different from that of soldiers, being extremely elegant and strongly influenced by French fashions: black kepi with dark blue bottom band, having golden quarter-piping (according to rank) and chinstrap. It also bore a golden unit badge on the front (a "chasseur" horn). Grey double-breasted tunic with golden buttons and unit badge on the collar. Dark blue collar and piping to pointed cuffs. Grey trousers with golden piping, black leather knee-high boots. Rank was shown by golden shoulder bars and Hungarian knots on the sleeves. The outfit was completed by a golden waistbelt.

National Guard Infantry Battalion "Atacama": the original uniform of this battalion was supplied by the inhabitants of Copiapó, where the unit was raised. The businessmen of the city paid all the expenses for the equipment and uniforms of the battalion; the latter, curiously for the Chilean Army, were black[67]. As a result of this peculiar colour, the soldiers of the "Atacama" Battalion soon became known as "padrecitos" (which means "little priests"). The complete outfit of the "Atacama" was as follows: entirely black kepi, bearing brass unit badge (consisting of the letters "B" and "A" with a Chilean star in the middle). Black double-breasted or single-breasted long tunic with brass buttons, having red collar and round cuffs. Black trousers, buff leather boots. The brass buckle of the black leather waistbelt bore the Chilean star surrounded by the inscription "GUARDIA CIVICA DE COPIAPO". For the Lima campaign the unit received conventional 1880 campaign dress.

National Guard Infantry Battalion "Aconcagua": curiously this unit had a red kepi with dark blue bottom band like that of the regulars, but this bore the brass unit badge of the Civic Guard (a Chilean star) on the front. Dark blue single-breasted short jacket with brass buttons, having red piping to front and bottom edges. Red collar and round cuffs. Grey trousers, buff leather boots.

EQUIPMENT

The equipment carried by the Chilean soldiers were heavily modified during the war, in order to make them more effective for use on campaign[68]. One of the first things to be modified was the backpack: the traditional one made of leather and employed before the war soon proved to be too heavy for long marches and thus was replaced by a new piece of equipment known as "mochila-cama". This was a rucksack that functioned also as a bed for the foot soldier. It consisted of a parallelogram of resistant canvas to which a wool blanket and a sheet of rag fabric were attached. At night its main body of canvas was opened and placed under the back of the soldier; the wool blanket was used as a pillow and the sheet of rag fabric was used to cover the soldier's body. Despite initial expectations, the new rucksack was not extremely loved by soldiers, who generally preferred using the universal canvas bag instead of it. The old leather backpack, instead, continued to be used in large numbers. The canvas haversack (known as "morral"), which did not exist before the war and started to be produced only since 1879, was very simple but extremely resistant. It was edged with brown leather and supported by a brown leather strap. The interior of this practical bag was divided longitudinally in two by a strip of canvas that allowed to separate food provisions from ammunitions. Very often the canvas haversack had a black inscription with the name of the soldier. Another piece of equipment that had to be changed, but this time more effectively, was the canteen (known as "caramañola" or "cantimplora"). The original model used before the war was cylindrical and made of thin, being very simple and designed for moderate climates (in fact it could carry only 1,5 litres of water). The hard reality of a war fought in the Atacama Desert obliged the Chilean high command to create a new model of canteen: this was made of tin as the previous one but could carry 2 litres of water. This was kidney-shaped, which made it more practical because it could lay flat against the side of the soldier.

The campaign equipment of cavalry and artillery included canvas haversack and tin canteen, in addition to a white leather crossbelt specifically designed for mounted and artillery units. This divided in two braces around the half: one sustained the black leather ammunition pouch on the back, while the other sustained the carbine. Before the war, ammunitions were carried by infantry soldiers in a simple black leather pouch

67 Greve-Moller P., Fernàndez-Cerda C., *Uniforms of the Pacific War 1879-1884*, Nottingham, 2010
68 Greve-Moller, Patricio, *Equipamiento Chileno en la Guerra del Pacifico 1879-1884*, Santiago, Chile, 2014

The famous "cantinera" Irene Morales Infante, a real Chilean heroine of the war.

attached to the waistbelt; very soon, however, the needs of war forced the Chilean soldiers to employ canvas cartridge belts (known as "cananas") in order to carry more ammunitions. These belts, having two straps, were produced in two versions: a simple one without hangers that could carry 100 rounds and a double one with hangers that could carry 200 rounds. In total 2,500 cartridge belts of the first kind and 15,000 of the second one was produced. The personal equipment of infantrymen was completed by other three minor elements: a cork to protect the muzzle of rifles from dust, a cover designed to preserve the delicate mechanisms of the weapons and a knife with curved blade. This, known as "corvo" or "cuchillo", was a tool traditionally used by Chilean miners for their work; during the war it was employed as a lethal weapon for hand-to-hand combat. During the Sierra campaign some Peruvian items of equipment were adopted, like the traditional "ojotas" that were very comfortable for long marches.

PLATE A: CHILEAN INFANTRY

A1: Captain, 3rd Line Infantry Regiment, 1879

This officer wears the parade dress prescribed by the 1878 dress regulations. Dark blue shako with golden quarter-piping showing rank; golden pompom and lace holder. National cockade, golden unit number, black leather top band, visor and chinstrap. Dark blue double-breasted tunic with golden buttons and unit number on the collar; red piping to collar, round cuffs and front. The buckle of the black leather waistbelt was decorated with a star (of the same kind depicted on the Chilean national flag). "Garance" red trousers with dark blue piping, black leather shoes. Rank was shown by golden epaulettes (with white fringes) or contre-epaulettes and by golden rings around the cuffs.

A2: Soldier, 1st Line Infantry Regiment, 1879

This soldier from the "Buín" Regiment wears the standard "guerrera" (campaign dress) employed on the field. Red kepi with dark blue bottom band and piping, bearing a brass unit number on the front and having black leather visor. Dark blue single-breasted short jacket, having brass buttons and red collar. Red piping to front and round cuffs. The unit number was reproduced also on the brass buckle of the black leather waistbelt. "Garance" red trousers with dark blue piping, black leather shoes. The main weapon is a Comblain II rifle, as for the other soldiers of this plate.

A3: Soldier, 5th Line Infantry Regiment, 1881

This soldier from the "Santiago" Regiment wears the new campaign dress introduced in 1880. Light blue-grey kepi with brass unit number on the front; light blue-grey double-breasted tunic with red collar and round cuffs, having brass buttons; entirely light blue-grey trousers and buff leather boots. The front of the tunic could be piped in red, but generally it was not. A brass unit number was frequently worn on the collar. The uniform of our soldier bears the typical tactical marks used for the Lima Campaign: three horizontal parallel stripes in white (showing this unit's belonging to the 3rd Division of the Chilean Army) and a red "S" with a vertical stripe (unit mark of the "Santiago" Regiment).

A4: Soldier, "Zapadores de la Frontera", 1879

The uniform of this unit was quite similar to that worn by the foot artillery. Dark blue kepi with red quarter-piping, brass unit badge on the front (a letter "Z") and black leather visor. Dark blue double-breasted short jacket with brass buttons; red piping to collar and round cuffs. Dark blue trousers with red double side-stripe, black leather shoes. The brass buckle of the black leather waistbelt bore the same unit badge worn on the kepi. Note the bayonet with serrated blade typical of this unit.

A5: Soldier, "Artilleria de Marina", 1879

This uniform of the Naval Artillery was introduced in 1877 and remained the same during the war. Dark blue kepi with grey bottom band and brass unit badge on the front (consisting of a crossed cannon-and-anchor under a star and within a circle of laurels). Dark blue double-breasted short jacket with brass buttons; grey collar, pointed cuffs and frontal piping. Yellow decorative piping to cuffs. Dark blue trousers with grey piping, buff leather boots. The brass buckle of the black leather waistbelt bore the same unit badge worn on the kepi.

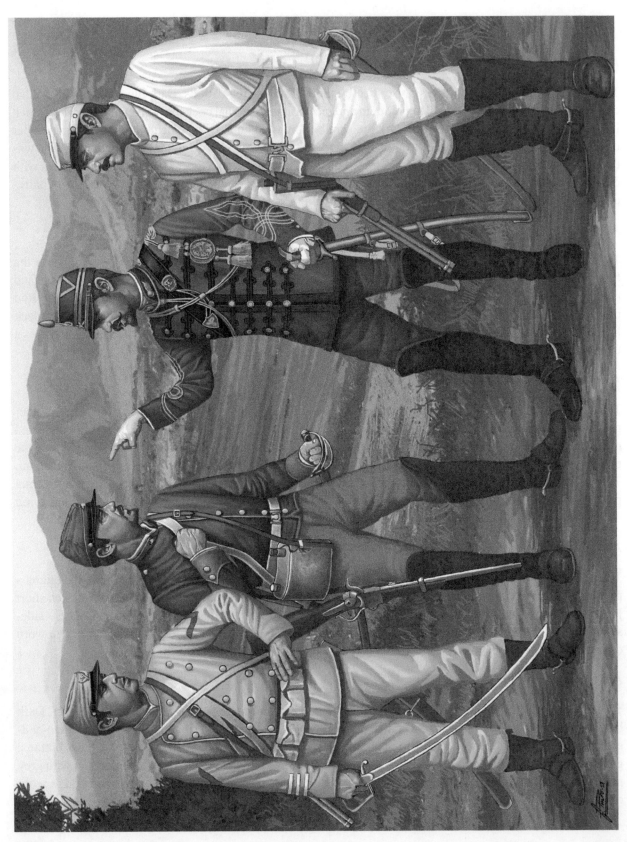

PLATE B: CHILEAN CAVALRY AND ARTILLERY

B1: Lieutenant, Mounted Company of the 1st Artillery Regiment, 1879

Uniforms of the horse artillery were very similar to those worn by cavalry. The parade dress of this officer is extremely elegant and rich, as prescribed by the 1878 dress regulations. Dark blue shako with single golden "chevron" on each side, national cockade and golden top band. Golden pompom and lace holder, black leather visor and golden chinstrap. Golden unit badge on the front, consisting of a flaming grenade over two crossed cannons. Golden rank piping around the base of the shako. Dark blue dolman with black frontal frogging and three rows of golden buttons. Frontal and bottom edges in black, collar and pointed cuffs piped in red. Golden unit badge on the collar. Dark blue trousers with red double side-stripe, black leather boots and black belts. Rank was shown by golden Hungarian knots on the sleeves and by golden shoulder boards. Additional golden cords and flounders were worn.

B2: Trooper, "Cazadores a Caballo" Regiment, 1879

This cavalry soldier wears the "guerrera" used by mounted units. "Garance" red kepi with green bottom band and quarter-piping; brass unit badge on the front, consisting of a "chasseur" horn. Chinstrap and visor were in black leather. Dark blue single-breasted stable jacket with brass buttons; green frontal piping, collar and pointed cuffs. Brass unit badge on the collar. "Garance" red trousers with green piping, black leather boots and white leather belts. Weaponry consists of a French M1839 Chatellerault saber and M1860 Spencer carbine.

B3: Trooper, "Granaderos a Caballo" Regiment, 1880

For summer, Chilean soldiers (from either foot or mounted units) could use this specifically designed tropical uniform: it was made of linen or drill, being entirely white. It consisted of a short single-breasted jacket with brass buttons and trousers. Also the kepi was covered in white, but had a brass unit badge on the front (in this case a flaming grenade). Weaponry consists of a French M1839 Chatellerault saber and M1866 Winchester carbine.

B4: Trooper, "Carabineros de Yungay" Regiment, 1881

This trooper wears the cavalry version of the new campaign dress introduced in 1880. Light blue-grey kepi with brass unit badge on the front (a crossed saber-and-carbine within a circle of laurels); light blue-grey short jacket with three rows of brass buttons, having collar and pointed cuffs in the distinctive colour of each unit (light blue for the "Carabineros de Yungay"); entirely light blue-grey trousers with light blue piping and buff leather boots. The front of the jacket could be piped in the colour of the unit, but generally it was not. The uniform of our soldier bears the typical tactical marks used for the Lima Campaign: three horizontal parallel stripes in white (showing this unit's belonging to the 3rd Division of the Chilean Army) and a red "V" (unit mark of the "Carabineros de Yungay" Regiment). This cavalry unit was the only in the Chilean Army to wear divisional marks on the cuffs. Weapons are an old British M1796 light cavalry saber and M1866 Winchester carbine.

PLATE C: CHILEAN NATIONAL GUARD

C1: Sub-lieutenant, "Navales" Battalion, 1879

Officers of this unit were dressed as their equivalents of the Chilean Navy (with uniforms copied from the contemporary dress regulations of the Royal Navy). Their uniform was as follows: dark blue peaked cap with golden chinstrap, quarter-piping (according to rank) and unit badge on the front (an anchor surrounded by laurels). Dark blue double-breasted frock-coat with golden buttons and dark blue step collar. Rank was shown by golden rings around the cuffs and golden shoulder bars. White shirt and black tie. Dark blue trousers and black leather shoes.

C2: Sub-lieutenant, "Cazadores del Desierto" Battalion, 1880

The outfit of this unit's officers was quite different from that of their soldiers, being extremely elegant and strongly influenced by French fashions. Black kepi with dark blue bottom band, having golden quarter-piping (according to rank) and chinstrap. It also bore a golden unit badge on the front (a "chasseur" horn). Grey double-breasted tunic with golden buttons and unit badge on the collar. Dark blue collar and piping to pointed cuffs. Grey trousers with golden piping, black leather knee-high boots. Rank was shown by golden shoulder bars and Hungarian knots on the sleeves. The outfit was completed by a golden waistbelt.

C3: Soldier, "Bulnes" Battalion, 1879

The uniform depicted here was donated to this battalion by one of the richest Chilean women of the time, Isidora Goyenechea, who guided a real industrial empire in her country. Kepi having white cover and neck curtain, with a letter "B" written in black on the front. Medium blue single-breasted jacket with brass buttons; dark blue collar and round cuffs. Brass unit badge on the collar (a letter "B"). Medium blue trousers, buff leather boots. The brass buckle of the black leather waistbelt was decorated with a Chilean star encircled by the inscription "GUARDIA MUNICIPAL DE SANTIAGO". The rifle is a M1874 Gras.

C4: Soldier, "Chacabuco" Battalion, 1879

When formed in Santiago, at the beginning of the war, this elite National Guard unit received a very peculiar uniform that included the Peruvian "Pickelhaube" helmets confiscated in Valparaiso. The captured helmets were soon modified in order to have a Chilean star on the frontal plate instead of the Peruvian national shield. They were later given to 1st "Antofagasta" Battalion when the "Chacabuco" adopted ordinary kepis. The rest of this battalion's uniform was as follows: dark blue single-breasted jacket with brass buttons, having green collar, round cuffs and frontal piping. White trousers with green piping, black shoes. The rifle is a M1874 Gras, which was used by the majority of the Mobilized National Guard units during the first two war campaigns.

PLATE D: THE PERUVIAN ARMY IN 1879

D1: Sergeant, 2nd Line Infantry Battalion "Zepita", 1879

This elite battalion, the best infantry unit of the army, was the only to have the privilege of wearing a red kepi among Peruvian foot troops. Our soldier is dressed in campaign uniform according to the 1863 dress regulations. Red kepi with dark blue bottom band, brass unit number on the front, black leather visor and chinstrap. Dark blue single-breasted jacket with light blue piping to collar, round cuffs and front. Brass buttons and unit number on collar. "Garance" red trousers with light blue piping; white gaiters and black shoes. Rank was shown by inverted "chevrons", which were red for corporals and yellow for sergeants. The rifle is a M1866 Chassepot.

D2: Soldier, 4th Line Infantry Battalion "Callao", 1879

This soldier wears the standard summer/tropical uniform used by the Peruvian infantrymen during the first two war campaigns; this could be made of rag fabric (locally known as "bayeta") or of canvas (locally named "loneta"). The headgear is the classic "bonnet de police" locally known as "cristina" or "coscacho": with the summer dress this was white with red pompom and light blue piping. The rest of the uniform was as follows: white single-breasted jacket having light blue piping to collar, round cuffs and front; white trousers piped in light blue and black shoes. Light blue was the distinctive piping colour of the Peruvian infantry. The rifle is a Comblain II.

D3: Trooper, "Húsares de Junín" Regiment, 1879

This elite regiment, the best cavalry unit of the army, was with no doubts one of the most important units of the Peruvian military forces. During the War of the Pacific it fought wearing the uniform prescribed for cavalry by the 1863 dress regulations. Red kepi with dark blue bottom band and piping, with brass unit badge on the front (an Inca sun) and white neck curtain. Dark blue single-breasted jacket with red collar and brass buttons. Red piping to round cuffs and front. Red trousers with double side-stripes and black leather boots. Weapons are an old British M1796 light cavalry sabre and M1866 Winchester carbine.

D4: Trooper, "Lanceros de Torata" Regiment, 1879

This unit was dressed in the new cavalry uniform introduced by the 1872 dress regulations. "Pickelhaube" (spiked helmet) with brass frontal plate representing the Peruvian national shield and Peruvian national cockade. Dark blue single-breasted coatee with red piping to collar, pointed cuffs, frontal and bottom edges. Brass buttons. The collar bore a brass unit badge, consisting of crossed palm-and-sabre. Dark blue trousers with red piping and black leather boots. The sabre is an old British M1796 light cavalry one.

D5: Soldier, 1st Artillery Regiment "2 de Mayo", 1879

Our artilleryman wears the pre-war uniform prescribed by the 1863 dress regulations: dark blue kepi with red piping and brass flaming grenade on the front. Dark blue double-breasted tunic with red piping to collar, pointed cuffs and front. Brass buttons and flaming grenades on collar. Red trousers with black piping, black shoes. The rifle is a Comblain II, since Peruvian artillerymen were armed as normal infantrymen.

PLATE E: THE PERUVIAN ARMY IN THE LIMA CAMPAIGN

E1: Soldier, 6th Infantry Battalion of the Reserve, 1881

As all the infantry battalions of the "Army of the Reserve", this unit has not a name but just a number. Our soldier is wearing the new simple campaign uniform introduced by Piérola with the dress regulations of 12 July 1880. Dark blue kepi with white metal unit number on the front; dark blue single-breasted or double-breasted (like in this case) jacket, with white piping to collar, round cuffs, front and bottom edges. Dark blue trousers with white piping, white gaiters and black shoes. Buttons of the jacket could be brass or white metal; very frequently jacket and trousers had no piping. The rifle is a M1874 Turkish Peabody-Martini.

E2: Soldier, Artillery Brigade of the Reserve, 1881

The new dress regulations of 12 July 1880 prescribed the following simple uniform for artillery soldiers of the "Army of the Reserve": light blue-grey kepi with red flaming grenade on the front, light blue-grey single-breasted jacket with red collar and piping to front and pointed cuffs. Light blue-grey trousers with red piping, white gaiters and black shoes. Our artilleryman is armed with a M1873 Winchester carbine.

E3: Soldier, "Guarnición de Marina" Battalion, 1881

The soldiers of this elite unit had a very distinctive and elegant uniform, while the officers were dressed as their equivalents of the Peruvian Navy (with uniforms copied from the contemporary dress regulations of the Royal Navy). Dark blue shako with golden chinstrap, having golden naval emblem on the front (consisting of the Peruvian national shield over two crossed anchors) and a pompom (half white and half red, divided vertically) sustained by a golden button. Dark blue tunic with red collar, pointed cuffs and frontal piping. White metal buttons, golden shoulder bars with a decorative anchor. The collar had dark blue patches bearing a golden anchor. White trousers piped in red, white gaiters and black shoes. Note the many black leather ammunition pouches for the Comblain II rifle.

E4: Soldier, 83rd Line Infantry Battalion "Ayacucho", 1881

This unit was formed by Colonel Miota together with the cavalry "Morochucos de la Muerte" and its men had the same ethnic origin of the more famous "gauchos" (being of mixed Indian and Spanish descent). The soldiers of this unit had a very peculiar uniform, different from the usual one worn by all the other infantry units of the "Army of the Line": it had been made by the women of Ayacucho with coarse fabric and had a large Inca sun embroidered in gold on the back of the jacket (worn as a sort of "protection" for soldiers). Black kepi with brass unit number on the front; black single-breasted jacket with brass buttons and light blue piping to collar, front and round cuffs. Black trousers with light blue piping and black shoes. The rifle is a "Castañon" one.

E5: Policeman, "Columna Policía de Seguridad de Lima", 1881

The policemen of Lima, as all the other Peruvian ones, were dressed in black. Their uniform was quite simple: entirely black kepi with white metal unit badge on the front (depicting the heraldic shield of Lima). Entirely black single-breasted frock-coat with brass buttons; entirely black trousers and shoes. Our policeman is armed with a Comblain II rifle.

PLATE F: THE PERUVIAN ARMY IN THE SIERRA CAMPAIGN

F1: Captain of the Infantry, Army of the Centre, 1883

During the fourth war campaign Peruvian officers tended to use what uniforms they already had or could buy, but with the progression of time a certain degree of uniformity was achieved. The standard uniform of the officers from the Army of the Centre was as follows: dark blue kepi with red bottom band, golden unit badge on the front (an Inca sun) and golden quarter-piping (according to rank). Dark blue double-breasted frock-coat with red collar and pointed cuffs. Brass buttons, golden shoulder bars and inverted "chevrons" on cuffs (according to rank). White trousers with large red side-stripes and black shoes or boots.

F2: Soldier, 5th Infantry Battalion "Huancayo", Army of the Centre, 1881

The regular units of the Army of the Centre gradually adopted a red kepi as universal headgear: this could have a white curtain for protection of the neck and was sometimes worn also by the irregular groups of Quechua "guerrilleros". With the few funds at his disposal Cáceres tried to dress his battalions with coarse cotton cloth (locally known as "tocuyo asargado") in sea green colour. However, due to the chronic economic restrictions, only the 5th Infantry Battalion "Huancayo" received this new uniform. Red kepi with brass unit badge on the front (an Inca sun); sea green single-breasted jacket with red collar and pointed cuffs, having brass buttons. Sea green trousers and black shoes. The rifle is a "Castañon" one.

F3: Soldier, 2nd Line Infantry Battalion "Cajamarca", Army of the North, 1883

The infantrymen of Iglesias' Army of the North initially had no uniform, wearing simple white jackets and trousers. To differentiate his men from those of Cáceres' Army, Iglesias ordered them to wear an entirely dark blue kepi. When Iglesias' small army transformed itself into the new "Regenerating Army", it started to receive formal assistance by the Chileans: as a result, the Chilean General Supply Corps sold uniforms and equipment to the Army of the North at very good conditions and prices. Iglesias, however, was also able to conclude a contract with the Grace Brothers Company in the USA for the acquisition of surplus campaign uniforms from the stores of the Unionist Army (surplus from the US Civil War). As a result, the 2nd Line Infantry Battalion "Cajamarca" wore the American uniform depicted here: dark blue kepi with brass unit number on the front; entirely dark blue single-breasted jacket with brass buttons; light blue trousers, white spats and black shoes. The rifle is a "Castañon" one.

F4: Morochuco Montonero, 1883

The Morochucos, who had already fought during the third war campaign before as light cavalry and later as sappers, continued to give their contribution to the Peruvian war effort during the Sierra Campaign. Their traditional clothing usually included slouch hats (as in this case) or fur caps. The most traditional element of their outfit was the colourful "poncho". Some of them had sabers, but the majority was armed with lances. Note the red band worn around the hat, typical of Cáceres' irregulars.

F5: Breñero Quechua, 1883

The irregular "guerrilleros" from the mountain villages of the Quechua Indians were dressed in their traditional civilian clothing, which was not so different from that of the Morochucos. Note the use of a red kepi, the only uniform item worn by this fighter. The rifle is a M1874 Peabody-Martini. The small bands of Indian "guerrilleros" were generally armed with a variety of weapons including traditional spears, javelins and slings; they also employed agricultural tools used as improvised weapons like axes, pitchforks and machetes.

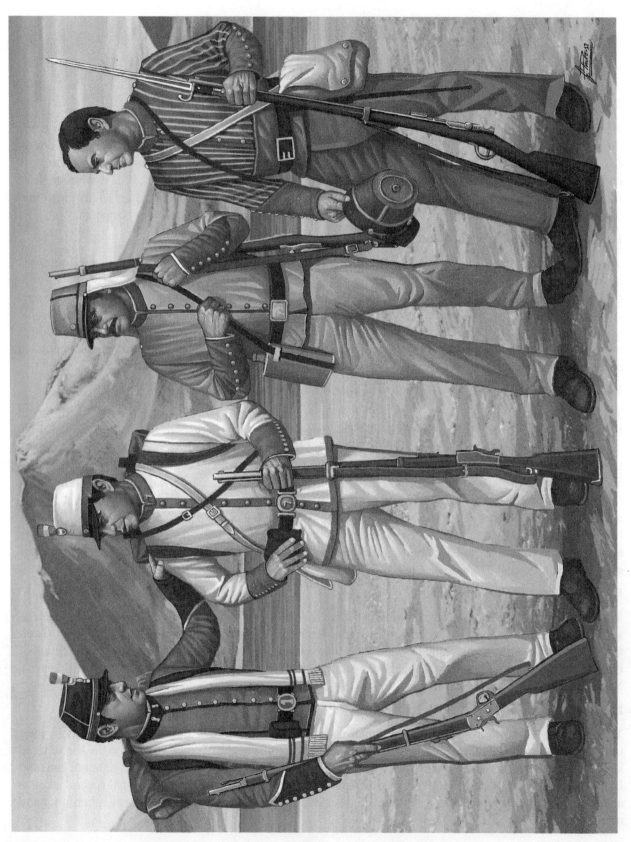

PLATE G: BOLIVIAN INFANTRY

G1: Soldier, 1st Line Infantry Battalion "Daza", 1879

This soldier of the elite "Colorados" Battalion, the best infantry unit of the Bolivian Army, wears the standard campaign dress received in 1879 for the first war campaign. This uniform shows some of the Bolivian infantry dress' most characteristic features: jacket having colour from the Bolivian national flag, deep slanting cuffs and a profusion of decorative buttons on the sleeves. Formally the "Colorados" were a unit of grenadiers and this was reflected in their unit badge, which was a flaming grenade. Black kepi with green bottom band and yellow piping, having brass flaming grenade on the front and national cockade. Pompom in national colours, black leather visor and chinstrap. Red jacket with black collar and slanting cuffs; black piping to front and bottom edges. White piping to the cuffs, brass flaming grenades on the collar. White trousers with black side stripes. Note the number "1" on the brass buckle of the black leather waistbelt. Differently from the other two regular battalions, the "Colorados" had two lines of additional black piping on each side of the jacket (which passed on the shoulders and continued also on the back). The "Colorados" Battalion, as well as the "Sucre" and "Illimani" ones, was easily recognizable thanks to the use of a white scarf with three decorative horizontal stripes in red (known as "bufanda"). These scarves were not employed by the new units formed after the declaration of war, so they soon became a distinctive feature of the regular battalions. According to a contemporary Chilean chronicler, the red cloth of the "Colorados" uniforms was of excellent quality, having been bought by Daza in 1876 from the French merchant Guillot, who was established in La Paz. Apparently, this red cloth was surplus supply coming from France, having been formerly used to produce the uniforms of the Imperial Guard. Bullhide sandals (known as "ojotas") were frequently preferred to black leather shoes on campaign, because they were very comfortable for long marches. The elite "Colorados" were armed with the excellent 11mm M1871 Remington rolling-block rifle.

G2: Soldier, 7th Line Infantry Battalion "Tarija", 1879

The uniform reproduced here is a good example of the campaign dress worn by the new Bolivian infantry units formed in 1879. White kepi with red bottom band, cockade and pompom in national colours, brass decorative button on the front, black leather visor and chinstrap. White jacket with red collar and slanting cuffs; red piping to front and bottom edges. Brass unit number on collar and on the buckle of the black leather waistbelt. White trousers with red side stripes, black shoes. The rifle is a M1871 Remington.

G3: Soldier, National Guard Infantry Battalion "Independencia" (3rd of La Paz), 1879

Like the three regular infantry battalions, the three National Guard ones formed in La Paz had red, yellow and green as distinctive colours: their uniforms were grey but had facings in the Bolivian national colours (red for the "Victoria", yellow for the "Paucarpata" and green for the "Independencia"). Grey kepi with green piping, brass decorative button on the front, white neck cover, black leather visor and chinstrap. Grey jacket with green collar, slanting cuffs and frontal piping. Grey trousers with green side stripes, black shoes. Our soldier is armed with a M1871 Remington.

G4: Soldier, National Guard Infantry Battalion "Columna Loa", 1879

This was the first uniform worn by this battalion, which was formed with Bolivians living in the Peruvian province of Tarapacá who worked in the local nitrate mines. Red kepi with dark blue bottom band and yellow piping; brass decorative button on the front, black leather visor and chinstrap. Dark blue blouse with white vertical stripes; red collar, slanting cuffs and frontal piping. Dark blue trousers with red side stripes, black shoes. This uniform was nothing else than the working dress used by the Bolivian miners in southern Peru, with the addition of some military elements. The rifle is a "Castañon" one.

PLATE H: BOLIVIAN CAVALRY AND ARTILLERY

H1: Sub-lieutenant, Line Cavalry Squadron "Escolta" (1st of Cuirassiers), 1879

The uniform of this squadron was the most elaborate one of the Bolivian Army and was designed (like the unit itself) on the model of Napoleon III's "Cent-Gardes". In fact, the helmets and cuirasses of this squadron were imported from France as surplus items of the disbanded French Imperial Guard. Once dispatched to Bolivia, the helmets and cuirasses of the "Cent-Gardes" were modified in order to have a more Bolivian appearance. The Bolivian national shield was added to the front of the helmet, while an Inca Sun was added on the breastplate. The steel helmet had brass crest, visor and chinscales; black mane, red tuft and plume. The steel breastplate and backplate were joined by brown leather shoulder straps, with white metal buckles attached to the brass decorations. A protective lining of red cloth, known as "fraise", was worn under the cuirass. The uniform was produced by French tailors established in Bolivia, according to Daza's personal taste. It consisted of a yellow jacket with green collar and slanting cuffs, the collar being piped in yellow. Rank was shown by the use of golden epaulettes and contre-epaulettes. Trousers were made of light grey cloth with darker grey vertical stripes; they also had red side-stripes. The tall black boots were of black leather. Pennons of the lances were in the Bolivian national colours and had golden decorative fringes. Members of this unit were equipped only with French-made sabers and lances, because having a purely ceremonial function.

H2: Trooper, Line Cavalry Squadron "Bolívar" (1st of Hussars), 1879

The uniform of the Bolivian Hussars was similar to that of the Chilean "Granaderos a Caballo", thus leading to some confusion on the field of battle. It consisted of red kepi with dark blue bottom band and piping, having black leather visor and chinstrap. The kepi had a brass device on the front (an Inca Sun) and was frequently worn together with a white protective cover for the neck. Dark blue jacket with red piping to collar, slanting cuffs and front. Brass buttons. Red trousers with dark blue side stripes, tall black boots. Weaponry consists of a French-made sabre and M1865 Spencer carbine.

H3: Trooper, Volunteer Cavalry Squadron "Rifleros del Norte" (1st of the Bolivian Legion), 1879

As with the other two squadrons that made up the "Bolivian Legion", this unit used two different uniforms. The first one (represented here) consisted of black kepi with green top band and piping; black jacket with green collar, slanting cuffs and piping to the front and bottom edges, having green frogging on the front. Brass buttons. Black trousers with three green side stripes, tall black boots. The only weapon is a M1871 Remington carbine.

H4: Sub-lieutenant, Artillery Regiment "Santa Cruz", 1880

The service uniform of Bolivian infantry and artillery officers was very simple and practical, being intended for use on campaign: it could be single-breasted or double-breasted (like in this case) but had more or less the same features. Entirely dark blue kepi with golden rank piping and artillery badge (a flaming grenade) on the front. Golden chinstrap, black visor and white neck cover. Dark blue double-breasted tunic, having golden epaulet-loops on the shoulders and inverted rank "chevrons" on the sleeves. Golden buttons and flaming grenades on collar. Dark blue trousers with red side stripes and black shoes.

155

LIST OF ILLUSTRATIONS

Picture 1: Admiral Juan Williams Rebolledo, commander of the Chilean Navy until August 1879.

Picture 2: The monitor Huáscar as it is today, after complete restoration.

Picture 3: Contemporary photo of the Chilean fleet at the beginning of the war.

Picture 4: Painting showing the sinking of the Chilean "Esmeralda" during the battle of Iquique.

Picture 5: Painting showing the crucial moments of the decisive naval clash at Angamos.

Picture 6: Clash between Chilean and Peruvian soldiers at the battle of Arica (7 June 1880).

Picture 7: The USS warship "Lackawanna", on which indecisive peace talks took place in 1880.

Picture 8: Admiral Patricio Lynch, commander of the Chilean occupation forces in Peru.

Picture 9: General Baquedano, commander of the Chilean Army from April 1880 to May 1881.

Picture 10: Contemporary photo showing the entrance of the Chilean infantry in Lima.

Picture 11: Colonel Estanislao del Canto, commander of the first Chilean expedition in the "Sierra".

Picture 12: Map of the War of the Pacific

Picture 13: Hilarión Daza Groselle, dictator of Bolivia from 1876 to 1879.

Picture 14: General Narciso Campero, President of Bolivia from January 1880 until 1884.

Picture 15: M1871 Remington

Picture 16: The mechanism of the US M1860 Spencer carbine, employed by the Bolivian cavalry.

Picture 17: Gatling machine gun, employed by all the armies involved in the conflict.

Picture 18: Soldier of the "Sucre" Battalion; note the protectors of coarse cloth and bullhide sandals.

Picture 19: Soldier of the "Columna Loa" Battalion, wearing this unit's second uniform. Drawing by Benedetto Esposito.

Picture 20: Trooper of the Line Cavalry Squadron "Bolívar", also known as "1st of Hussars". Drawing by Benedetto Esposito.

Picture 21: Bolivian mounted volunteers, dressed with civilian clothes like the "Franco Tiradores".

Picture 22: Trooper of the "Rifleros del Centro" Squadron, wearing this unit's first uniform. Drawing by Benedetto Esposito.

Picture 23: The "Rifleros del Sur" Squadron; rankers are wearing this unit's second uniform.

Picture 24: Map showing the region of Antofagasta in the Atacama Desert.

Picture 25: Mariano Ignacio Prado Ochoa, President of Peru during 1876-1879.

Picture 26: The Peruvian Admiral Miguel Grau Seminario, commander of the Huáscar.

Picture 27: Nicolás de Piérola Villena, dictator of Peru from December 1879.

Picture 28: Map of Lima, showing the port of Callao and the island of San Lorenzo.

Picture 29: Map showing the Peruvian defensive lines of Chorrillos and Miraflores, south of Lima.

Picture 30: Francisco García-Calderón, provisional President of Peru during March-November 1881.

Picture 31: Admiral Lizardo Montero Flores, legitimate President of Peru from November 1881.

Picture 32: General Cáceres, leader of the Peruvian resistance forces during the fourth war campaign.

Picture 33: General Miguel Iglesias, "regenerating" President of Peru from January 1883.

Picture 34: General Buendía, commander of the Allied Army during the first war campaign.

Picture 35: The mechanism of the French M1866 Chassepot rifle, employed by Peru.

Picture 36: Photo of a M1874 Turkish Peabody-Martini rifle, employed by Peru.

Picture 37: Colt M1873, used by Chilean and Peruvian officers as a privately-purchased weapon.

Picture 38: Soldier, National Guard Infantry Battalion "Guarnición de Marina". Drawing by Benedetto Esposito.

Picture 39: Lieutenant of the 2nd Line Infantry Battalion "Zepita", wearing M1863 service dress. Drawing by Benedetto Esposito.

Picture 40: Soldier, 2nd Line Infantry Battalion "Cajamarca" from Iglesias' Army of the North. Drawing by Benedetto Esposito.

Picture 41: Soldier of the 2nd Line Cavalry Regiment "Lanceros de Torata", wearing M1872 uniform. Drawing by Benedetto Esposito.

Picture 42: Trooper, National Guard Cavalry Column "Gendarmes de Tacna". Drawing by Benedetto Esposito.

Picture 43: Gunner, Artillery Brigade of the Reserve, battles for the defence of Lima. Drawing by Benedetto Esposito.

Picture 44: Map showing in detail the territorial acquisitions obtained by Chile from Peru and Bolivia.

Picture 45: Aníbal Pinto Garmendia, President of Chile during 1876-1881.

Picture 46: Chilean officer wearing campaign dress and equipment, including a traditional "corvo".

Picture 47: The Chilean General Staff; note the use of white tropical pith helmets made of cork.

Picture 48: Emilio Sotomayor Baeza, one of the most important and experienced Chilean officers.

Picture 49: Chilean Staff officers; in the background there are cavalrymen with M1852 parade dress.

Picture 50: Municipal Guardsmen from Santiago, wearing their pre-war uniforms in French style.

Picture 51: Captain of the 1st National Guard Infantry Battalion "Antofagasta".

Picture 52: Soldier of the National Guard Infantry Regiment "Valparaiso", wearing M1880 campaign dress with divisional and unit marks. Note the canvas belts for carrying ammunitions.

Picture 53: Colonel of the National Guard Infantry Regiment "Chacabuco".

Picture 54: Captain of the National Guard Infantry Regiment "Chacabuco", in campaign dress.

Picture 55: The "Chacabuco" at the beginning of the war, with grey greatcoats and Peruvian helmets.

Picture 56: Officers and soldiers of the National Guard Infantry Battalion "Navales".

Picture 57: Lieutenant of the National Guard Infantry Regiment "Lautaro".

Picture 58: Soldier of the National Guard Infantry Regiment "Atacama".

Picture 59: Captain of the National Guard Infantry Battalion "Caupolicán".

Picture 60: Soldiers of the "Esmeralda" Regiment in skirmishing formation during training.

Picture 61: Lieutenant and sergeant of the "Esmeralda"; the NCO is wearing the grey greatcoat.

Picture 62: Officers and soldiers of the National Guard Infantry Regiment "Chillán".

Picture 63: Lieutenant of the National Guard Infantry Regiment "Melipilla".

Picture 64: Sergeant of the National Guard Infantry Regiment "Aconcagua".

Picture 65: Sub-lieutenant of the National Guard Infantry Regiment "Concepción".

Picture 66: Lieutenant of the National Guard Infantry Regiment "Talca".

Picture 67: Captain of the National Guard Infantry Regiment "Talca" with campaign equipment.

Picture 68: Captain of the "Talca" Regiment with captured Peabody-Martini rifle.

Picture 69: Captain of the National Guard Infantry Battalion "Rengo".

Picture 70: Officers and flag of the National Guard Infantry Battalion "Victoria".

Picture 71: Captain of the National Guard Infantry Battalion "Quillota".

Picture 72: Sergeant of the National Guard Infantry Battalion "Quillota".

Picture 73: Sub-lieutenant of the National Guard Infantry Battalion "Lontué" in service dress.

Picture 74: Officers of the National Guard Infantry Battalion "Lontué".

Picture 75: Chilean sergeant in summer campaign dress, with buff desert boots and white trousers.

Picture 76: Chilean officers of the 1st Line Infantry Regiment "Buín".

Picture 77: Chilean captain of the 1st Line Infantry Regiment "Buín".

Picture 78: Sergeant of the 1st Line Infantry Regiment "Buín"; the kepi is a National Guard one.

Picture 79: Chilean officers of the 2nd Line Infantry Regiment.

Picture 80: Soldiers of the 2nd Line Infantry Regiment, with "guerrera" and white-covered kepi.

Picture 81: Chilean officers of the 2nd Line Infantry Regiment in service dress.

Picture 82: Chilean sub-lieutenant of the 3rd Line Infantry Regiment in campaign dress.

Picture 83: Chilean soldiers of the 3rd Line Infantry Regiment in service dress.

Picture 84: Chilean officers of the 4th Line Infantry Regiment.

Picture 85: Chilean lieutenant-colonel of the 4th Line Infantry Regiment.

Picture 86: Officer of the 4th Line Infantry Regiment with the traditional Chilean "corvo" (knife).

Picture 87: Chilean officers of the 5th Line Infantry Regiment "Santiago".

Picture 88: Photo showing Chilean soldiers on the field, during a pause in the combat operations.

Picture 89: Contemporary drawing showing the entrance of the Chilean cavalry in Lima.

Picture 90: Colonel Alejandro Gorostiaga, Chilean divisional commander at Huamachuco.

Picture 91: The mechanism of the excellent Belgian Comblain II rifle, employed by Chile.

Picture 92: A Chilean battery of the 2nd Artillery Regiment, with Krupp M1879 field guns of 75mm.

Picture 93: Two Gatling machine guns manned by Chilean gunners of the 2nd Artillery Regiment.

Picture 94: Chilean lieutenant of the Naval Artillery Regiment.

Picture 95: The Line Cavalry Regiment "Granaderos a Caballo".

Picture 96: Trooper of the "Granaderos a Caballo" Regiment, wearing "guerrera". Drawing by Benedetto Esposito.

Picture 97: Corporal of the "Cazadores a Caballo" Regiment, with M1852 uniform.

Picture 98: Corporal of the "Cazadores a Caballo" Regiment, with M1852 parade dress. Drawing by Benedetto Esposito.

Picture 99: Ensign of the "Cazadores a Caballo" Regiment wearing service dress. Drawing by Benedetto Esposito.

Picture 100: Lieutenant of the "Granaderos a Caballo" Regiment, wearing M1878 parade dress.

Picture 101: Sergeants of the "Carabineros de Yungay" (right and left) and ensign of the "Cazadores a Caballo" (centre), respectively in campaign and service dress according to the 1878 dress regulations. The carbine is a captured Remington one.

Picture 102: Corporal of the "Carabineros de Yungay" Regiment wearing service dress.

Picture 103: Chilean artilleryman wearing the pre-war M1852 parade uniform.

Picture 104: Chilean colonel from the 1st Artillery Regiment in parade dress.

Picture 105: Officers from the mounted company of the 1st Artillery Regiment in parade dress.

Picture 106: Officers from the 1st Artillery Regiment wearing service or parade uniform.

Picture 107: Soldier from the 1st Artillery Regiment with M1878 service dress.

Picture 108: Soldier from the 2nd Artillery Regiment with M1878 service dress.

Picture 109: Officers of the 2nd Artillery Regiment wearing campaign uniforms.

Picture 110: Officers of the 2nd Artillery Regiment wearing campaign dress.

Picture 111: The famous "cantinera" Irene Morales Infante, a real Chilean heroine of the war.

Soldier from the 2nd Artillery Regiment, with service dress and divisional marks. Drawing by Benedetto Esposito.

Captain of the National Guard Infantry Regiment "Talca" with campaign uniform. Drawing by Benedetto Esposito.

Soldier of the National Guard Infantry Battalion "Navales" with campaign dress. Drawing by Benedetto Esposito.

SELECT BIBLIOGRAPHY

PRIMARY SOURCES

Barros-Arana, Diego, *Historia de la guerra del Pacífico 1879–1880*, Santiago, Chile, 1881

Bulnes, Gonzalo, *Chile and Peru: the causes of the war of 1879*, Santiago, Chile, 1920

De Varigny, Charles, *La Guerra del Pacifico*, Santiago, Chile, 1920

Gutierrez, Hipólito, *Crónica de un soldado de la Guerra del Pacífico*, Santiago, Chile, 1956

Paz-Soldan, Mariano F., *Narracion Historica de la Guerra de Chile contra Peru y Bolivia*, Buenos Aires, Argentina, 1884

SECONDARY SOURCES

Basadre, Jorge, *Historia de la Republica del Peru*, La guerra con Chile, Lima, Peru, 1964

Curtis, Alan, *To the last cartridge*, Nafziger Collection, 2007

Ejército del Peru, *Evolucion Historica de los Uniformes del Ejército del Peru (1821-1980)*, Lima, Peru, 2005

Esposito, Gabriele, *Armies of the War of the Pacific 1879-1883*, Oxford, 2016

Estado Mayor General del Ejercito, *Historia del Ejercito de Chile*, Santiago, Chile, 1980-1983

Farcau, Bruce W., *The Ten Cents War: Chile, Peru and Bolivia in the War of the Pacific*, London, 2000

Fernandez-Asturizaga, Augusto, *Uniformes Militares Bolivianos 1827-1988*, La Paz, Bolivia, 1991

Greve-Moller, Patricio, *Crónica del Chacabuco 6° de Línea,* Santiago, Chile, 2010

Greve-Moller, Patricio, *Equipamiento Chileno en la Guerra del Pacifico 1879-1884*, Santiago, Chile, 2014

Greve-Moller, Patricio, *La Caballeria Boliviana en la Guerra del Pacifico 1879-1884*, Santiago, Chile, 2013

Greve-Moller P., Fernàndez-Cerda C., *Uniformes de la Guerra del Pacifico 1879-1884*, Santiago, Chile, 2008

Greve-Moller P., Fernàndez-Cerda C., *Uniforms of the Pacific War 1879-1884*, Nottingham, 2010

Instituto de Estudios Histórico-Marítimos del Perú, *Historia marítima del Perú*, Lima, Peru, 2004

Lòpez-Urrutia, Carlos, *La Guerra del Pacifico 1879-1884*, Madrid, 2003

Peri-Fagerstrom, René, *Los Batallones Bulnes y Valparaiso en la Guerra del Pacifico*, Santiago, Chile, 1980

Querejazu-Calvo, Roberto, *Guano, Salitre y Sangre*, La Paz, Bolivia, 1979

Rosales, Justo A., *Mi campaña al Perú*, 1879–1881, Concepciòn, Chile, 1984

Sater, William F., *Andean Tragedy: Fighting the War of the Pacific 1879–1884*, University of Nebraska, 2007

Sater, William F., *Chile and the War of the Pacific*, University of Nebraska, 1986

Scheina, Robert L., *Latin America's Wars: The age of the caudillo 1791–1899*, Potomac Books, 2003

Lieutenant-colonel of the "Carabineros de Yungay" Regiment, in parade dress.

Captain of the National Guard Infantry Regiment "Talca", with red unit mark.

Sub-lieutenant of the National Guard Infantry Regiment "Esmeralda" in campaign dress.

INDEX

Sergeant of the 1st Line Infantry Regiment
"Buín", wearing campaign dress ("guerrera").

Lieutenant of the National Guard Infantry
Regiment "Chacabuco", in service dress.

The National Guard Infantry Regiment
"Esmeralda" at the beginning of the war.

Sub-lieutenant of the National
Guard Infantry Regiment "Talca".

BIOGRAPHIES

Gabriele Esposito is a military historian who works as freelance author and researcher for some of the most important publishing houses in the sector of military history. In particular, he is an expert specialized in uniformology: his interests and expertise range from the ancient civilizations to the modern post-colonial conflicts. During the last few years he has conducted and published several researches on the military history of the Latin American countries, with special attention to the War of the Triple Alliance and the War of the Pacific. He is among the leading experts on the military history of the Italian Wars of Unification and of the Spanish Carlist Wars. His books and essays are published on a regular basis by Osprey Publishing, Winged Hussar Publishing, and Pen & Sword; he is also the author of numerous military history articles appearing on specialized magazines, like *Ancient Warfare Magazine, Medieval Warfare Magazine, The Armourer, History of War, Guerres et Histoire, Focus Storia, Focus Storia Wars.*

Ángel García Pinto was born in Madrid in 1968. He finished his Fine Arts career at the Complutense Faculty of Madrid in the 90's. At that time he began to collaborate on a regular basis with one of the most important newspapers of Spain, *ABC*, making portraits of relevant personalities from the political, cultural and economic life of the moment. This stage lasted more than 15 years. During this period he also worked for the economic newspaper *Cinco Días*. A little later, he began to make illustration and design work in the field of advertising, as well as for textbooks. Subsequently, he began his specialization in Military History and for more than 20 years he has been collaborating to national and international publications, illustrating specialized magazines and books on different topics, from Ancient Rome to the Tercios of Flandes, from Ancient Greece to the Second World War, touching all epochs. He works for publishers from Spain, Netherlands, Portugal, USA, and Russia.

Soldier of the 4th Line Infantry Regiment, wearing standard campaign equipment.

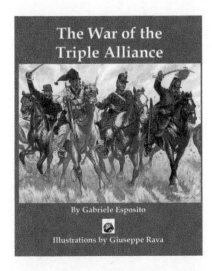

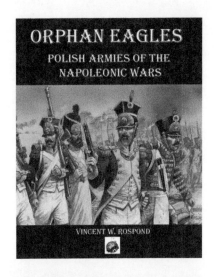

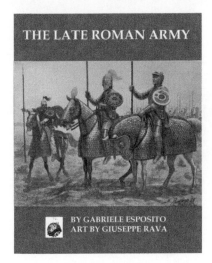

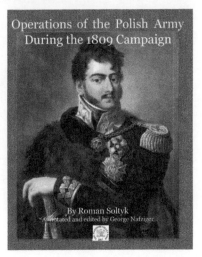

Look for more books from Winged Hussar Publishing, LLC
– E-books, paperbacks and Limited Edition hardcovers.
The best in history, science fiction and fantasy at:

www. wingedhussarpublishing.com

or follow us on Facebook at:Winged Hussar Publishing LLC

Or on twitter at:WingHusPubLLC

For information and upcoming publications